When Odysseus in his wanderings was cast up by the sea on the shores of Drepane, his first thoughts were: "To what country am I come? And what manner of people are here?" These are the perennial questions of the foreign visitor. How big is the country? What is the longest river, the biggest lake, the highest mountain? How many people are there? And how do they make their living? What has their history been like? What language do they speak? What arts do they admire?

Ireland—the Great Little Answerbook sets forth the answers to these and hundreds of other questions in relation to Ireland. By the liberal use of quotations from Irish writers it casts a glow of understanding around the facts. It also seeks, where possible, to relate Ireland to the visitor's own country. Thus it identifies the Irishman who became the father of the US Navy and who, after the British surrender at Yorktown in 1781, brought Lafayette back to France. It indicates that James Callaghan, British Prime Minister (1976-79), is one of the six million people of Irish descent who live in Britain. It names the place in Ireland where the father of the first president of Chile came from. It points out that Spain is Ireland's ninth most important trading partner and that the USA, the UK and Germany are by far the biggest overseas investors in Irish manufacturing industry.

Ireland—the Great Little Answerbook also acquaints you with the wide range of extraordinary facts that make Ireland such a fascinating country—how Ireland gave English the words "blarney", "boycott", "whiskey" and "galore"; how the bones of St Valentine, the patron saint of lovers, rest in a church in Dublin; how an Irishman and two Germans made the first east to west flight across the Atlantic; how, apart from Greece and Rome, Ireland has the longest continuous literary tradition in Europe; how one of the legendary classical Greek heroes visited Ireland; how leprechauns came to exist. It also tells you which Irish writer said, "Woman begins by resisting a man's advances and ends by blocking his retreat", and which said, "Do not do unto others as you would they should do unto you. Their tastes may not be the same".

It is notoriously difficult to present facts in an animated way. Those who seek to do so must be mindful of the stern reviewer of a history of Waterford who wrote, "The text is like the Sahara—dry and full of dates". *Ireland—the Great Little Answerbook* is presented in a question-and-answer format developed by Jim O'Donnell in *Wordplay* (Peartree Press, 1992).

USING THIS BOOK

1   The body of the text is presented in a question-and-answer format.
     Questions appear on a right hand page and the answers to them
     appear on the following left hand page.

2   To use the available space to best effect some questions are front-
     loaded with information and some answers are back-loaded.

3   Two outline maps of Ireland at the beginning of the book allow you
     to fix in your mind the Irish places and geographical features
     mentioned in the book. The first map sets forth the counties,
     provinces and Northern Ireland. The second locates cities, towns,
     rivers, lakes, mountains, cliffs, islands and regions.

4   A detailed index allows you to track down items of information
     quickly. Key words from quotations are given in Italic, as are the
     titles of books, plays, films, the names of ships and non-English
     words.

IRELAND

ATLANTIC
OCEAN

DERRY

DONEGAL

ANTRIM

TYRONE

ULSTER

DOWN

FERMANAGH

ARMAGH

MONAGHAN

SLIGO

LEITRIM

CAVAN

LOUTH

MAYO

ROSCOMMON

LONGFORD

MEATH

CONNACHT

WESTMEATH

LEINSTER

DUBLIN

GALWAY

OFFALY

KILDARE

IRISH
SEA

LAOIS

WICKLOW

CLARE

KILKENNY

CARLOW

TIPPERARY

WEXFORD

LIMERICK

MUNSTER

WATERFORD

KERRY

CORK

NORTHERN IRELAND

v

IRELAND

PLACES, RIVERS, LAKES, MOUNTAINS, CLIFFS, ISLANDS & REGIONS MENTIONED IN THE TEXT

CONTENTS

QUESTION 1

The population of Ireland is approximately
(a) 1.5 million?
(b) 3 million?
(c) 5 million?

QUESTION 2

Oscar Wilde (1854-1900) was born in Dublin, educated in Portora, Enniskillen, Co. Fermanagh, Trinity College Dublin and Oxford. A brilliant epigrammatist, he wrote plays of enduring genius. His lecture tour of America in 1882 was a great success. In the town of Leadville, high up in the Rocky Mountains, he read to the miners, who mined for silver, extracts from the autobiography of the Florentine Benvenuto Cellini (1500-71), perhaps the greatest of silversmiths. "I was reproved by my hearers for not having brought him with me. I explained that he had been dead for some little time which elicited the inquiry, 'Who shot him?' " In one of his plays, Wilde observed, "*No woman should ever be quite accurate about her age. It looks so calculating*".
Was it in   (a) *Lady Windermere's Fan*?
              (b) *The Importance of Being Earnest*?
              (c) *A Woman of No Importance*?

QUESTION 3

The Irish climate is so temperate that the wind storm of exceptional severity which swept the country on the evening and night of 6 January 1839 still lives in folk memory as the Night of the Big Wind (*Oíche na Gaoithe Móire* in Irish). However, Irish weather (the day-to-day meteorological conditions affecting a specific place), as distinct from climate (the long-term pattern of weather conditions in a region), is unfailingly variable, a matter which may account for the Irish interest in the weather as a topic of conversation; and for the fact that the annals written in Irish monasteries from the sixth to the twelfth centuries provide the earliest weather records in Europe. We know from them that Armagh, the ecclesiastical capital of Ireland, was devastated by an appalling thunderstorm in 995, during which the round tower was destroyed by lightning and a general conflagration laid waste much of the city and its surrounding forest. On this event the annalists pronounced, "There came not in Ireland since it was discovered, and there never will come again until the Day of Judgment, a vengeance like it".
    The introduction of scientific measurement has given modern Ireland's weather reports a much less colourful cast. The first organised weather recording in Ireland was established at Dunsink, Co. Dublin. In what year was this achieved?
Was it in   (a) 1788?
              (b) 1790?
              (c) 1845?

ANSWERS OVERLEAF

1

ANSWER 1

(c) 5 million. Of these, 3.5 million live in the Republic and 1.5 million live in Northern Ireland. The population of Scotland, Sicily, Denmark and Finland is also 5 million each. Belgium, Greece and Portugal have populations twice as large. The Netherlands has a population three times as large. The population of Spain is eight times Ireland's, that of Britain and France eleven times, that of Germany sixteen times, that of Japan twenty-five times and that of the USA fifty times. In the European Union (EU), one out of every 68 people is Irish.

Modern Ireland is relatively sparsely populated. In the 1840s, Ireland's population reached its highest level of 8.5 million. (At that time England and Wales had 16 million, Italy 22 million and Germany 30 million; if Ireland's population had increased proportionately to that of the rest of Europe, it would now be about 20 million.) In the 1840s, most Irish people depended for their food on a single crop, the potato, introduced from the New World to Ireland about 1600 AD. In the period 1845-48, blight struck the potato crop, turning the healthy plant to a black, withered stalk and quickly causing the potatoes to rot in the ground. The Famine that resulted was the greatest catastrophe in Western Europe in several hundred years. A million people died and a flood of emigrants—to Britain, Canada and especially to the USA—put Ireland's population into a decline through emigration that was not reversed until the 1960s.

The Famine turned Ireland into one of the world's great mother countries—some 60 million people throughout the world today (about twelve in every thousand) claim Irish ancestry. Vivid memories of the horrors of the Famine explain the exceptional response of Irish people to famine—in the Sudan, Ethiopia and Somalia.

ANSWER 2

(b) *The Importance of Being Earnest.* After his disgrace and imprisonment in Britain, Wilde fled to France. Debt-ridden and impoverished, he said to the doctor who asked for a large fee for an operation, "I suppose that I shall have to die beyond my means". He is buried in Père Lachaise cemetery in Paris; his grave is marked by a monument by Jacob Epstein (1880-1959).

ANSWER 3

(a) 1788. Recording was established at Armagh in 1790 and at Birr in 1845. Birr has another claim on the attention of science: in 1845, too, the Earl of Rosse established a giant telescope, in the grounds of his castle at Birr, to explore the galaxies. The telescope was the largest in the world until the beginning of the twentieth century.

QUESTIONS ON PREVIOUS PAGE

QUESTION 4

Up to about four hundred years ago Ireland was covered in trees. But when the original Irish land owners were dispossessed, the new occupants, uncertain of their title should the Stuarts be restored to the English throne, felled much of the timber to secure some return from their estates while the going was good. They also cut down forests to deprive the dispossessed owners of refuges from which to harry the new settlers. The phenomenal population growth in the early nineteenth century also contributed to the clearing of woodlands. By 1900, only 1% of the country was under forest, an unbelievably low figure. In the European Union as a whole, 26% of land is under trees.

A fragment of Ireland's once extensive oak woods still survives at Coolattin in Co. Wicklow, near the village of Shillelagh. The shillelagh, a name applied to the blackthorn cudgel wielded by faction fighters in the eighteenth century, was originally a stout oak stick, large quantities of which came from the woods of Shillelagh. Also in Co. Wicklow is the Glen of the Downs, a spectacular glacially-formed ravine, whose slopes are clothed in naturally growing forest, a rare sight in Ireland. Irish reafforestation began in 1904 when the government bought Avondale, the Wicklow estate of the late Irish leader, Charles Stewart Parnell, for the purpose. What percentage of land in the Republic is now under trees?

> Is it   (a) 5%?
>   (b) 7%?
>   (c) 15%

QUESTION 5

Anagram: F O R B U T E A
The scale of wind velocities

QUESTION 6

What Irish-born person said, "*Marriage is popular because it combines the maximum of temptation with the maximum of opportunity* "?

> Was it   (a) George Bernard Shaw?
>   (b) Patrick Brontë, father of the Brontë sisters?
>   (c) Cecil Day-Lewis?

QUESTION 7

Which classical hero, according to Greek legend, visited Ireland?

> Was it   (a) Hercules (Heracles) in the course of his twelve labours?
>   (b) Ulysses in the course of his wanderings on the way home from Troy?
>   (c) Jason on his return from Colchis with the Golden Fleece?

ANSWER 4

(a) 5%

ANSWER 5

Beaufort. The Beaufort scale, the international scale of wind velocities, was devised by Sir Francis Beaufort (1774-1857), admiral in the British Royal Navy, who was born at Navan, Co. Meath. He was descended from Huguenots who had settled in Ireland less than a hundred years before his birth. The Beaufort bag, the familiar air-sock flown at airports to indicate the direction of the wind, is also called after him.

ANSWER 6

(a) George Bernard Shaw. Shaw (1865-1950) was antipathetic to the whole spirit of the Celtic Revival in the late nineteenth and early twentieth centuries. He explained his reason for leaving Ireland at a time of cultural renaissance thus: "I too might have become a poet like Yeats, Synge and the rest of them. But I prided myself on thinking clearly, and therefore could not stay. Whenever I took a problem or state of life of which my Irish contemporaries sang sad songs, I always pursued it to its logical conclusion, and then inevitably it resolved itself into comedy. That is why I did not become an Irish poet... I could not stay there dreaming my life away on the Irish hills. England had conquered Ireland, so there was nothing for it but to come over and conquer England".

There is a relatively small number of artists whose power and genius call into being an enduring adjectival form of their names. In Ireland there are six, all of them writers: Swift (Swiftian), Wilde (Wildean), Yeats (Yeatsian), Joyce (Joycean), Shaw (Shavian), and Beckett (Beckettian).

ANSWER 7

(c) Jason. In a poem attributed to Orpheus, Jason reached the northern ocean and visited Ireland (Ierne in Greek) before returning home through the Pillars of Hercules (Gibraltar). A third-century AD Latin writer, Adrianus Junius, speaks of "icy Ierne" as being well known to the Greeks of old and to Jason and the Argonauts. Swift refers to the legend in his poem "On the Sudden Drying Up of Saint Patrick's Well Near Trinity College Dublin, 1726":

> *Ierne, to the world's remotest parts*
> *Renowned for valour, policy and arts,*
> *Hither, from Colchis with the fleecy ore*
> *Jason arrived two thousand years before.*

QUESTION 8

Where is Ireland's first wind farm situated?
    Is it in   (a) Co. Donegal?
                (b) Co. Mayo?
                (c) Co. Cork?

QUESTION 9

The Irish word *Dáil* means "assembly". Dáil Éireann means "the Assembly of Ireland" and describes the Republic's house of representatives. There are 166 *Teachtaí Dála* (Dáil deputies; a deputy is referred to as a TD). Ireland has a bicameral legislature—Denmark has the only unicameral legislature in the EU. The upper house—the Senate—is called Seanad Éireann. How many members has it?
            Is it   (a) sixty?
                     (b) eighty?
                     (c) a hundred?

QUESTION 10

A survey carried out in 1972 for the International Union for the Conservation of Nature and Natural Resources identified the outstanding landscapes in the Republic. What percentage of the area of the state did it classify as of outstanding natural beauty?
        Was it   (a) 16.6?
                  (b) 17.6?
                  (c) 18.6?

QUESTION 11

Anagram: G H O U L R T U
A dry lake

ANSWER 8

(b) Co. Mayo. Opened at Bellacorick by a Danish company, the farm is set to produce 17 million units of electricity per annum, thereby taking out of circulation about 13,000 tonnes of carbon dioxide (CO_2) per annum which would otherwise be produced by generating the electricity from fossil fuel. Carbon dioxide emissions from fossil fuels in Ireland, in terms of CO_2 per head of population, are among the lowest in the European Union. In earlier times wind-power was harnessed directly by windmills. The largest windmill in working order in Ireland or Britain may be seen in Blennerville, outside Tralee, Co. Kerry.

ANSWER 9

(a) sixty

ANSWER 10

(b) 17.6. Britain at 16.7% was almost as high. The re-discovery of Nature by the Romantic movement led Europeans to express a preference for mountainous landscapes described by the words "wild", "remote", "natural", "untamed", "unspoiled". Altitude also makes cliffs their most favoured coastal landscape. It is not surprising, therefore, that the West of Ireland, on the western rim of Europe, with its mountains, cliffs, lakes and forests, should have so strong a romantic appeal. Killarney in Co. Kerry, "heaven's reflex" in the remote south-west, is fabled as the most beautiful place in Ireland. It is interesting to note that one of the earliest methods of classifying and evaluating landscapes was derived from Edmund Burke's *Philosophical Enquiry into the Origin of Our Ideas of the Sublime and the Beautiful* (1756).

ANSWER 11

Turlough. If, during the winter, you are driving west of the Shannon in Galway or Mayo, you may be puzzled by the existence of lakes which do not appear on the half-inch Ordnance Survey maps. If you look more closely, you may wonder why some of them have stone walls running down into them or even telegraph poles in the middle of them. These are turloughs, literally "dry lakes" in Irish. They appear and disappear with the seasons. They are a geographical phenomenon unique to Ireland. They are confined to limestone areas where there is only a thin covering of soil over the rock. The rainfall in consequence disappears through the porous limestone to flow to the sea through underground channels. In winter, however, the subterranean system is unable to cope with the increased flow and the excess water is forced temporarily to the surface in low-lying areas, thereby forming turloughs.

QUESTION 12

Radio Telefís Éireann is the Republic's national broadcasting service. Its radio transmissions began in 1926, its television transmissions in 1961. It depends for its revenue on income from licence fees (the current colour television licence fee is IR£62) and sales of advertisements and of the *RTE Guide*. Radio services are also provided by more than twenty commercial or community local/regional stations. There are over 1,000,000 television homes in the state. How many of these have colour receivers?

Is it   (a) seventy-three per cent?
        (b) eighty-three per cent?
        (c) ninety-three per cent?

QUESTION 13

Anagram: D E E R L A M
A peculiarly Irish stone?

QUESTION 14

John Millington Synge (1871-1909) wrote plays of extraordinary imagination and musicality. "In a good play", he said, "every speech should be as fully flavoured as a nut or apple". In *The Playboy of the Western World*, Christy Mahon assures Pegeen, "*It's little you'll think if my love's a poacher's or an earl's itself, when you'll feel my two hands stretched around you, and I squeezing kisses on your puckered lips, till I'd feel a kind of pity for the Lord God is all ages sitting lonesome in His golden chair* ". This classic play was made into a film starring Siobhán McKenna and Garry Redmond in what year?

Was it   (a) 1952?
        (b) 1962?
        (c) 1972?

QUESTION 15

Who said, "*Ireland could be reduced and held by a single legion and a few auxiliaries*"?

Was it   (a) Julius Caesar, who led the first Roman invasion of Britain with six legions in 55 BC?
        (b) Agricola, a first-century AD Roman governor of Britain?
        (c) Hadrian, who built the famous wall against the Picts between 122 and 127 AD?

ANSWER 12

(c) ninety-three per cent

ANSWER 13

emerald. The emerald is a green-coloured semi-precious stone. "The Emerald Isle" was first used as a name for Ireland by the Northern poet William Drennan (1754-1820): *"Nor one feeling of vengeance presume to defile/The cause or the men of the Emerald Isle"* (from his poem "Erin"). Various semi-precious stones are present in Ireland in small amounts. They include amethyst, azurite, beryl, garnet, malachite, topaz and smoky quartz—but not emerald.

ANSWER 14

(b) 1962

ANSWER 15

(b) Agricola (40-93 AD), quoted by his son-in-law, the historian Tacitus. The Romans never invaded Ireland. Indeed, Irish raids hastened their departure from Britain in the early part of the fifth century. In one such raid a teenage boy was captured and carried off to Ireland. After a number of years he escaped home, but he was drawn back to Ireland to convert the pagans there to Christianity. His mission was so successful that he is still honoured today as St Patrick, the patron saint of Ireland.

Christianity brought writing to Ireland. (The druids had developed a script called Ogham but it was suitable only for short, monumental epitaphs.) A literary culture in Irish, based on the orally transmitted sagas and poetry, rapidly developed. Apart from Greece and Rome, Ireland, for this reason, has the longest continuous literary tradition in Europe. Christianity also created a vigorous monastic culture that produced an astonishing range of world-class artistic achievements in stone-work, metal-work and illuminated manuscripts.

Because the Romans never conquered Ireland, Ireland escaped the total civic disorder which followed the disintegration of their empire. The lamp of learning was kept burning in Ireland, and Irish monks and scholars, in one of the greatest cultural endeavours known to history, carried it bravely and indefatigably across Western Europe to light the way out of the Dark Ages (*c.* 600-1000 AD).

One of these personalities has no Irish ancestry. Which one?

President John F. Kennedy (1917-1963). His great-grandparents on his father's side were from Wexford, and on his mother's side from Limerick.

Charles de Gaulle (1890-1970) The French President was descended on his mother's side from the McCartans of Co. Down. The McCartan ancestor was an officer who fled to France after 1690.

Paul Keating (1944-) Australian Prime Minister (1991-). His grandfather came from Tynagh, Co. Galway.

Che Guevara (1928-1967), Cuban revolutionary, was born in Argentina. He was descended from Patrick Lynch, who fled to Spain from Ireland and then went to Argentina.

James Callaghan, now Baron Callaghan of Cardiff (1912-) British Prime Minister (1976-1979). He was born in Portsmouth, England. His father was born in Ireland.

Princess Grace of Monaco (1929-1982). Her father was a building contractor in Philadelphia whose parents came from Mayo. Her mother was an American of German extraction.

Marshal Timoshenko (1895-1970). Nobody, alas, has yet traced a tincture of Irish blood in the genetic inheritance of the Soviet hero.

Leopoldo O'Donnell (1809-1867), Spanish Prime Minister (1856-57, 1860-63, 1866-67). He was descended from a first cousin of the great Donegal chief, Red Hugh O'Donnell.

Brian Mulroney (1939-) Canadian Prime Minister (1984-93). His parents were born in Ireland.

Newgrange, the great megalithic tomb in Co. Meath, at the winter solstice. Is there an older building in the world?

The Custom House, Dublin, the masterpiece of the English architect, James Gandon (1742-1823).

Poulnabrone dolmen, the Burren, Co. Clare. Dolmens are the earliest megalithic tombs found in Ireland. They comprise three or four stone uprights supporting a large capstone. They are found in western Europe, especially in Brittany and westwards to the Aran islands. The word dolmen means 'stone table' in Breton.

QUESTION 16

The words of "It's A Long Way to Tipperary", probably the most popular song in World War I, were written by an Irishman, Jack Judge (1878-1938). Tipperary is the name of both a town and a county. In which of the four provinces of Ireland will you find it?

Is it in   (a) Ulster?
             (b) Leinster?
             (c) Connacht?
             (d) Munster?

QUESTION 17

Irish farming is predominantly pastoral—cattle in the lush plains, sheep on the hillsides. Thus livestock and livestock products, such as milk, butter and cheese, dominate the economy of the sector. The perennial importance of cattle in Ireland's economy is attested to by the fact that one of the earliest Irish sagas is called *Táin Bó Cuailnge* ("The Cattle-raid of Cooley") and involves an almost Homeric cast of kings and queens, nobles and champions. That work, incidentally, gives us a marvellous view of the world of the Iron Age Celts and corroborates much of what the Roman writers tell us about the life and temperament of the Celts, whom they encountered in Spain, France and Britain. There are more cattle in the Republic than there are people.

Is the number of cattle
             (a) 4 million?
             (b) 6 million?
             (c) 7 million?

QUESTION 18

The cliffs of Moher in Co. Clare form an impressive rampart against the Atlantic Ocean. They extend for a distance of 8km at a uniform height of almost 180 metres (600 feet). Although a majestic sight, they are not the highest cliffs in Ireland. Are the highest cliffs at
             (a) Mount Brandon in Co. Kerry?
             (b) Croaghaun on Achill Island, Co. Mayo?
             (c) Slieve League in Co. Donegal?

QUESTION 19

Of the 166 members of the twenty-seventh Dáil 20 are women. Of these, two are members of the cabinet and three are Ministers of State (junior Ministers). Of the 16 departments into which the Irish civil service is divided how many are headed by women civil servants?

Is it   (a) 4?
          (b) 2?
          (c) 1?

ANSWER 16

(d) Munster. Another of the best-known World War I songs, "Over There" (1917), was written by the Irish-American entertainer George M. Cohan (1878-1942), the father of American musical comedy.

ANSWER 17

(c) 7 million (1992)

ANSWER 18

(b) Croaghaun on Achill Island. The cliff face drops sheer to the sea from a height of 668 metres (2,192 feet). This is the highest cliff in north-western Europe (the spectacular cliffs at Slieve League, Co. Donegal, are 601 metres—1,972 feet—high). The highest cliff in Britain, on the island of St Kilda, is 400 metres (1,397 feet) high. The highest cliffs in the world, at 1,010 metres (3,300 feet), are on the Hawaiian island of Molokai.

ANSWER 19

None. The participation rate of Irish women in the labour market is 30%, the lowest in the EU (1993). Women predominate in low paid, low status occupations, which provide little opportunity for advancement. Their average earnings are 80% of those of men (but they work shorter hours). A marked feature of the participation of women in the Irish labour force is the high percentage of part-time workers who are female (70%). Thanks to a vigorous feminist movement, the position of women in the economic and social spheres is steadily improving. Thus there is (1994) a woman among the judges of both the Supreme and High Courts, and on the board of the Central Bank of Ireland. The director of the National Library of Ireland is a woman. In the political field a woman leads one of the mainstream political parties; and indeed, in percentage terms, the number of women TDs places Ireland sixth (1993) among the EU legislatures. Moreover the election of Mrs Mary Robinson as President of Ireland has given fresh inspiration to all who wish to ensure equal opportunities for women.

QUESTION 20

Anagram: L N D B O A G
A soft place

QUESTION 21

What is "Tyndall blue"?
Is it   (a) a rowing honour gained in University College Dublin?
        (b) the colour of the sky in daylight?
        (c) a type of dye formerly used on Kinsale cloaks, which were worn traditionally in Kinsale to about the middle of the twentieth century?

QUESTION 22

The Oscar awards are presented annually by the Academy of Motion Picture Arts and Sciences, Hollywood, for excellence in film production. In the form of statuettes, they derive their name, the story goes, from Oscar Pierce, an American corn-grower, on the basis of a chance resemblance to him. The name Oscar, now found world wide, as, for example, in the names of Oscar Hammerstein and the martyred Archbishop Oscar Romero of San Salvador, is Irish. It first came into prominence, in modern times, with the accession of Oscar I (1779-1851) to the throne of Sweden and Norway in 1844. Born in Paris, he was the son of Charles XIV of Sweden, formerly one of Napoleon's marshals, Jean-Baptiste Bernadotte, and Desirée Clary, a descendant of Irish emigrés in France.

At the time of his birth, the romantic movement was at its zenith in western art, literature and music. Romanticism was a rejection of classicism with a re-emphasis on the relationship of human beings to the natural environment. One of the main contributors to Romanticism was the Scot James Macpherson (1736-96) whose alleged translations from the "Gaelic or the Erse language" (i.e. Irish) in the 1760s fuelled the movement. Entitled *The Works of Ossian*, they became popular with European writers such as Goethe and Schiller, and also with Napoleon. It is not so surprising then that Bernadotte and his wife christened their first-born Oscar, after the son of Ossian, the legendary Irish hero. Perhaps coincidentally, Sir William Wilde, father of Oscar Wilde (probably the most famous bearer of the name), was a friend of Oscar II of Sweden. Oscar Wilde's mother was herself steeped in the romanticism of Irish folklore ("He is to be called Oscar Fingal Wilde", she wrote to a Scottish friend. "Is not that grand, misty, Ossianic?"). Appropriately, so far as the Oscar awards are concerned, the name Oscar in Irish means "champion" or "hero". When were the first Oscar Awards made in Hollywood?
Was it in   (a) 1927?
        (b) 1929?
        (c) 1931?

ANSWER 20

Bogland. Peatlands originally covered more than 17% of the land area of Ireland—a higher proportion than any other European country except Finland. Peat, or "turf" as it is more commonly called in Ireland, formed after the last Ice Age, about ten thousand years ago. It consists of the partially rotted and partially preserved debris of roots, leaves, flowers, heathers, seeds, grasses and sedges that once grew in shallow, badly-drained depressions in the central lowlands. Peatlands, with their unique eco-system, are a seriously endangered habitat of flora and fauna throughout Western Europe. Ireland is one of the few countries where a wide range of peatlands still exists in an almost natural state. Nevertheless, owing to the mechanical exploitation of this fuel source, out of an original 1,200,000 hectares of peatland, only about 100,000 hectares of scientific interest remain unscathed. Steps are being taken to conserve some 70,000 hectares as representative samples. A notable feature of peatland is its preservative character. Thus in a bog in Denmark the remarkably preserved body of a prehistoric man has been recovered. In his poem "The Tollund Man" Seamus Heaney avers:

> *Some day I will go to Aarhus*
> *To see his peat-brown head,*
> *The mild pods of his eye-lids,*
> *His pointed skin-cap.*

In Ireland the bogs frequently yield the roots of trees preserved for thousands of years. Exquisite carvings in bog-oak by Irish artists are available in craft shops. The word "bog" derives from the Irish *bog* "soft"

ANSWER 21

(b) the colour of the sky in daylight, so called after John Tyndall (1820-93), the eminent Carlow-born scientist who explained the molecular scattering which results in the sky's appearing blue in sunlight. Tyndall studied for his doctorate at the University of Marburg in Germany and, as a professor in the Royal Institution in London, he became a close friend of Faraday. He also showed that ozone was a naturally occurring gaseous variant of oxygen. Today he is credited with being the first to suggest that the "greenhouse effect" (a term of modern provenance) was a major factor in governing the temperature of the earth's surface.

ANSWER 22

(b) 1929, in the Blossom Room of the Hollywood Roosevelt Hotel. The Academy was founded in 1927.

QUESTION 23

Of all the islands in the world does Ireland rank in size

(a) twentieth?

(b) fifty-seventh?

(c) one hundred and ninth?

QUESTION 24

George Berkeley (1683-1753) was born in Co. Kilkenny and educated at Trinity College Dublin. An Anglican bishop of Cloyne (a diocese in Co. Cork), he was also a major philosopher, ranking as an empiricist with John Locke (1632-1704) and David Hume (1711-76). His fundamental thesis, 'being is being perceived', was popularly taken to mean that the physical world exists only in the mind. The debate which he initiated has not yet ended. In this century, it prompted the following limerick from a fellow divine and wit, Ronald Knox:

> *There once was a man who said 'God*
> *Must find it exceedingly odd*
> *If He finds that this tree*
> *Continues to be*
> *When there's no one about in the Quad.'*

This drew a riposte from an anonymous scribe:

> *Dear Sir, your astonishment's odd;*
> *I am always about in the Quad,*
> *And that's why this tree*
> *Continues to be*
> *As observed by yours faithfully, God.*

Berkeley, seat of a famous university in America, is named after the philosopher.

Is it in (a) Vermont?

(b) Virginia?

(c) California?

QUESTION 25

How many counties are there in Ireland?

Are there (a) twelve?

(b) twenty-two?

(c) thirty-two?

ANSWER 23

(a) twentieth. Ireland, with a total area of 84,000 sq km is a relatively large island. It is far larger than any of the islands in the Mediterranean—Sicily (the largest at 26,000 sq km), Sardinia or Crete, for example. Britain, the larger island between it and the mainland of Europe (the eighth largest in the world), and which comprises England, Scotland and Wales, has a total area of 231,000 sq km. Ireland is larger than Scotland (79,000 sq km) and four times the size of Wales (21,000 sq km). Within the European Union, Luxembourg (2,600 sq km), Belgium (31,000 sq km), the Netherlands (41,000 sq km) and Denmark (43,000 sq km) are all substantially smaller. Portugal (92,000 sq km.) is larger by a tenth. In relation to the USA, Ireland is twenty-six times the size of the smallest state, Rhode Island (3,144 sq km) and one-eighteenth the size of the largest, Alaska (1,531,000 sq km).

ANSWER 24

(c) California. The University of California at Berkeley is just outside San Francisco.

ANSWER 25

(c) thirty-two. The Normans invaded Ireland in 1169, arriving in Wexford from Wales at the invitation of an Irish sub-king in need of allies. They gradually imposed their system of counties on the country—the process began in the reign of King John (1199-1216) and was completed by the English only in 1606—the last county, Wicklow, coming into being when the power of the local Gaelic chiefs, O'Byrne and O'Toole, was overcome. Northern Ireland, a political term introduced by the British Government of Ireland Act, 1920, has six counties. However, the most northerly county of all, Donegal, is not in "Northern Ireland" but in the Republic. The counties are grouped into four provinces—Leinster, Munster, Connacht and Ulster. Ulster consists of the six counties in Northern Ireland (63% of the total area of the province) and three counties (37% of the area) in the Republic (Donegal, Cavan and Monaghan). In the Republic the county is the basic unit of local government. Each has an elected council; an unelected full-time career official, the county manager, directs and controls the day-to-day work of the county council. For administrative purposes, Tipperary is treated as two counties and Dublin as three.

QUESTION 26

The great satirist Jonathan Swift rests in St Patrick's Cathedral in Dublin, a place, his epitaph assures us, "where fierce indignation can no longer tear his heart". The romantic hero Robert Emmet (1778-1803) urged, at the end of the trial which condemned him to death, "When my country takes her place among the nations of the earth, then, and not till then, let my epitaph be written". But possibly the most memorable of Irish epitaphs is that of a poet:

> *Cast a cold eye*
> *On life, on death.*
> *Horseman, pass by!*

Is that poet   (a) Austin Clarke (1896-1974)?
                (b) Louis MacNeice (1907-1963)?
                (c) William Butler Yeats (1865-1939)?

QUESTION 27

Anagram: M I L K R I C E
There was a young lady...

QUESTION 28

In which of his works did the Irish orator Edmund Burke (1729-97) say, "...*to tax and to please, no more than to love and be wise, is not given to men* "?
        Was it   (a) *On the Sublime and the Beautiful*?
                  (b) *On American Taxation*?
                  (c) *The Present State of the Nation*?

ANSWER 26

(c) William Butler Yeats. Yeats died in the south of France but because of the war his body rested there until 1948 when the Irish government dispatched a naval vessel to bring it back to Ireland. Now, as he had wished,

> *Under bare Ben Bulben's head*
> *In Drumcliff churchyard Yeats is laid.*

ANSWER 27

limerick. The popular verse form probably takes its name from the county by the Shannon. Some of the earliest examples of limericks in modern literature are contained in a poem in Irish, "The County of Mayo", attributed to Micheál Ó Bruadair, a Mayoman executed for piracy in Santa Cruz in the seventeenth century, but the form was popularised by a school of poets writing in Co. Limerick in the eighteenth century. Many of their verses in this genre have been translated into English by James Clarence Mangan (1803-49). In Irish limericks the rhyme at the end of the third and fourth lines is repeated in the last line, as in this emended translation by Mangan of a limerick addressed in 1766 by one Limerick man to another, a publican who had written a limerick in praise of his own pub:

> *Dear Twomy, you count yourself handy*
> *At selling good ale and bright brandy,*
> *But the fact is your liquor*
> *Makes everyone sicker;*
> *You ought to be slicker, Yours, Andy.*

It was probably Mangan who gave the name "limerick" to this verse form.

ANSWER 28

(b) *On American Taxation.* By an eclectic process each of the two great political traditions of nineteenth century Britain—the Conservative and the Liberal—looks to Burke as the classical exponent of its principles. Burke's soaring rhetoric in defence of the American colonists asserted the claims of liberty against the despotism of George III; his reflections on the French Revolution upheld the claims of traditional authority against the despotism of the mob. Burke, who was averse to theories based on abstractions, is often contrasted with his contemporary Rousseau, whose explicitly political ideas are classical in their rationalism.

QUESTION 29

Of Asian origin, the bagpipes were introduced to Europe by the Romans. They were adopted by the Celtic peoples of Scotland, Ireland and Brittany, so much so that in Scotland they became a national symbol. Perhaps no other instrument can so plaintively convey lament. Thus Donald Cameron, who was a boy in the Highlands during World War II, recalls how his family responded to the sinking of a great battleship, on which his own cousin was lost: "We did not express our grief in words so much as in moods and music. On the night we heard about the *Royal Oak*, my father finished his work early and marched slowly up and down the horse park playing laments, one after another. The music blew sharply against the gathering darkness.... Our grief weighed oppressively and my father's pipe gave it voice".

The national organisation which promotes traditional Irish music (Comhaltas Ceoltóirí Éireann) owes its inception to the pipers' club (Na Píobairí Uilleann), which had its origins in the Liberties, in the heart of old Dublin, at the beginning of the twentieth century. What Irish musician has said, "*I got to try the bagpipes. It was like trying to blow up an octopus*"?

Was it   (a) Bob Geldof, the Boomtown Rat, who organised the Live Aid concert in 1985 to help the victims of famine in Ethiopia?

(b) Paddy Moloney of The Chieftains, probably the most famous group of Irish traditional musicians?

(c) James Galway, the flautist?

QUESTION 30

Which city has produced the greatest number of Nobel prizewinners for literature?

Is it   (a) Berlin?

(b) Dublin?

(c) Paris?

QUESTION 31

What is the total length of Ireland's coastline?

Is it   (a) 2,173 km?

(b) 3,173 km?

(c) 4,173 km?

ANSWER 29

(c) James Galway, a native of Belfast

ANSWER 30

(c) Paris. Since 1901, when the first award was made, up to and including 1992, six Parisians have won the prestigious award. They are Sully Prudhomme (1901), Anatole France (1921), Henri Bergson (1927), Roger Martin du Gard (1937), André Gide (1947), and Jean-Paul Sartre (1964). Sartre is unique in being the only winner voluntarily to decline the prize; the Russian Boris Pasternak initially accepted the 1958 award, but later refused it under pressure from the Soviet authorities. Next to Paris, Dublin has produced the most winners, these being William Butler Yeats (1923), George Bernard Shaw (1925), and Samuel Beckett (1969). Berlin has two winners to its name, Paul Heyse (1910) and Nelly Sachs; the latter shared the 1966 prize with Schmuel Josef Agnon of Jerusalem. Madrid, like Berlin, has had one outright winner, Jacinto Benevente (1922), and one joint winner, José Echegaray y Eizaguirre, who shared the 1904 prize with Frédéric Mistral of France. Of the remaining places throughout the world which produced a prizewinner six are also capital cities. They, and their prizewinners, are: Cairo (Naguib Mahfouz, 1988); London (Patrick White, 1973); Mexico City (Octavio Paz, 1990); Moscow (Boris Pasternak, 1958); Prague (Jaroslav Seifert, 1984) and Reykjavík (Halldór Laxness, 1955). New York, America's cultural capital, presents with Eugene O'Neill, who won in 1936.

ANSWER 31

(b) 3,173 km, a-gleam with numerous tawny strands including sixty-one international blue flag beaches; off the distant west coast, the Atlantic surges with effervescent delight, birds wheel above waves that flash with fish; further to sea whales tumble along one of their great oceanic pathways.... Ireland has kept itself largely free of pollution. The sea affords a natural barrier against animal-borne disease; thus Ireland, like Britain, is free of rabies. The quality of the Irish air is excellent. The prevailing westerly winds travel over thousands of miles of unpolluted ocean. There are no concentrations of heavy industry. There are no nuclear energy plants. The quality of the water is high. Almost 80% of inland waterways are unpolluted (salmon still spawn in Irish rivers) and only 1% is seriously polluted. There is a programme in place to eliminate entirely by the year 2000 pollution caused by sewage discharge by coastal towns.

Irish people have a profound love of their country, traditionally personified as a beautiful young woman in the *aisling* (vision) genre of poems. They also have a practical concern for a clean environment—they wish to maintain Ireland as the green larder of Europe.

QUESTION 32

In response to the need for transatlantic air services a seaplane base was established at Foynes in the Shannon estuary in the 1930s. Later, the belief that land-based aircraft would dominate post-war aviation led to the development of Shannon International Airport on the opposite side of the estuary. By an enactment of the Irish legislature in 1947 Shannon became the world's first duty-free airport. Another first for Shannon (in 1988) was the provision of immigration clearance facilities for passengers to the United States, facilities which obviate delays on arrival there.

Closely associated with Shannon is the invention of Irish (Gaelic) coffee, first proffered to an appreciative public by Bill Sheridan, the head chef at Foynes and subsequently Shannon. With the end of the Cold War, Shannon became an important stopover for Aeroflot flights to North and South America. When was Shannon Airport established?

Was it in   (a) 1939?
                 (b) 1942?
                 (c) 1946?

QUESTION 33

Irishmen have played a considerable role in modern maritime history. Thus, two of the following three countries regard an Irishman as the father of their navies.

Which are they:
                 (a) Argentina?
                 (b) Chile?
                 (c) United States of America?

QUESTION 34

This is the title of a play by an Irish author.
What is the missing word?
Deirdre of the _____ by John Millington Synge

QUESTION 35

Which Irish local newspaper became famous for keeping its eye on the Czar of Russia?

Was it   (a) *The Leinster Express*?
             (b) *The Limerick Chronicle*?
             (c) *The Skibbereen Eagle*?

ANSWER 32

(b) 1942. The first scheduled commercial flights through Shannon began in 1945. TWA, Pan Am and BOAC (now British Airways) all began operations through Shannon that year.

ANSWER 33

(a) and (c). Admiral William Brown (1779-1857), who broke the Spanish blockade of the River Plate in 1814 and freed Argentina, was born in Foxford, Co. Mayo. The Argentinian navy always names one of its chief warships after him. (Incidentally the largest community of people of Irish descent outside the English-speaking countries—about 300,000 people—is in Argentina. At one per cent of the total population, this community derives predominantly from post-Famine emigration from Counties Longford, Westmeath and Wexford.)

John Barry, who was born in Wexford, was appointed commodore of the fledgling US navy in 1797 by George Washington. A brilliant commander, Barry had provided the revolutionaries with a heartening success in 1776, when as captain of the *Lexington* he captured HMS *Edward*, the first British naval vessel taken by the rebels. After the fall of Yorktown in 1781, Barry was chosen to bring Lafayette, the French general who had gone to America in 1777 to fight for the Amercian cause, back to France.

ANSWER 34

Sorrows. JM Synge was born in Dublin. After studying at Trinity College, where he won prizes in Irish and Hebrew, Synge went to Paris to make his living by writing. In 1896 he returned to Ireland, at Yeats's suggestion, to steep himself in the speech of the common people and record a life never before described in literature. He wrote three masterpieces, *Riders to the Sea, The Playboy of the Western World,* and *Deirdre of the Sorrows.* In the preface to *The Playboy,* he gives a famous insight into how he followed Yeats's advice: "When I was writing *The Shadow of the Glen,* I got more aid than any learning would have given me from a chink in the floor of the old Wicklow house where I was staying, that let me hear what was being said by the servant girls in the kitchen".

ANSWER 35

(c) *The Skibbereen Eagle* (now no longer published). Skibbereen is a small town (population 2,300) in Co. Cork. The editor of *The Skibbereen Eagle* a hundred years ago was given to thundering no less loudly than his counterpart in *The Times* of London. In his most famous editorial (5 September 1898) he warned, "We will still keep our eye on the Emperor of Russia and on all such despotic enemies, whether at home or abroad, of human progression and man's natural rights".

QUESTION 36

The Burren ("a stony place" in Irish) in Co. Clare is a remarkable region, almost lunar in appearance. How extensive is it?

Is it   (a) 80 square miles (205 sq km)?
        (b) 120 square miles (308 sq km)?
        (c) 160 square miles (410 sq km)?

QUESTION 37

In the Garden of Remembrance in Parnell Square, Dublin, there is a sculpture which recalls one of the greatest stories of Irish folklore, the Children of Lir. Transformed by their jealous step-mother into swans, the children were destined to frequent desolate lake and sea wastes for almost a thousand years until released from their bondage by St Patrick. In addition to the rich store of tales in early Irish written sources, from the martial exploits of the pagan Fionn to the Atlantic explorations of the Christian St Brendan, Ireland possesses a wealth of popular tales handed down in a vibrant oral tradition. In terms of folklore Ireland is one of the most important countries in Europe. Historical factors have played a part in this, as well as the survival, down to quite recent times, of small communities along the western seaboard which had to rely on their own local resources for entertainment. Irish folklore embraces native tales and international stories, and sometimes a fusion of the two as in this Disneyesque episode in an adventure of the hero Fionn which recalls Odysseus' encounter with the one-eyed giant, Polyphemus:
"When the giant closed his one eye he began to snore, and every time he drew breath he dragged Fionn, the red-hot spit, the salmon on it and the goats to his mouth, almost swallowing them; and every time he released his breath, he drove them all back to the places where they were before. A blister arose on the partly-cooked salmon, and Fionn pressed it down with his thumb, hoping to conceal from the giant the harm that had been done. But he burnt his thumb, and to ease his pain put it in his mouth and sucked it. Immediately he received knowledge of all things (because he had tasted the Salmon of Knowledge). So the next time he was drawn up to the giant's face he knew what to do, and plunged the hot spit into the giant's sleeping eye and so killed him". Cúchulainn is another great hero of Irish folklore. Where in Dublin is there a statue of Cúchulainn?

Is it in   (a) the National Museum?
        (b) the General Post Office?
        (c) St Stephen's Green?

QUESTION 38

Anagram: V I N E L K
Thermodynamic genius

ANSWER 36

(c) 160 square miles. The region was formed by the scouring effect of Pleistocene ice-sheets (ten thousand and more years ago) on carboniferous limestone, resulting in bare fissured pavements of rock, below which exist underground caverns, rivers and lakes—a speleologist's paradise. Its hills are soil-less, treeless and waterless. Nowhere else in Ireland or Britain is there anything like this strange landscape. Its aspect impelled English poet laureate, John Betjeman (1907-84), to write:

> *Stony seaboard, far and foreign,*
> *Stony hills poured over space,*
> *Stony outcrop of the Burren,*
> *Stones in every fertile place.*

And yet in its sheltered nooks and crannies there is rich pasture and a profusion of flora. In May, in colourful display, there is a remarkable intermingling of plants belonging to the far north or alpine regions, such as mountain avens and spring gentians, and plants belonging to southern climes, like the close-flowered orchids, all of which here coexist right down to sea level. Paradoxically, human settlement has been continuous in this apparently barren region since the Neolithic era, about five thousand years ago.

ANSWER 37

(b) The General Post Office in O'Connell Street, which was the headquarters of the insurgents in the Easter Rising, 1916. The statue is by Oliver Sheppard (1864-1941).

A measure of Ireland's position in the world of folklore is the fact that the Department of Folklore in University College Dublin contains a million and a half manuscript pages of tales and traditions taken down directly from the lips of their tellers, apart from material recorded on tape and disc. Only Finland has a larger folklore collection.

ANSWER 38

Kelvin. William Thomson Kelvin (1824-1907), first Baron Kelvin, was born in Belfast, the second largest city in Ireland. A scientist and inventor of note in the fields of thermodynamics (the branch of physics concerned with the relationship between heat and other forms of energy), electricity and underwater telegraphy, he discovered the second law of thermodynamics (heat cannot be transferred from a colder to a hotter body within a system without net changes occurring in other bodies within that system). He is buried in Westminster Abbey, London.

Swift

Goldsmith

Wilde

Shaw

Yeats

Synge

Joyce

Behan

Beckett

Navan Fort (Eamhain Mhacha in Irish) was for six hundred years the residence of Ulster's prehistoric kings. A mound within the extensive fort is reputedly the burial place of Macha, an early Irish queen. Two miles away is Armagh, also called after her (Ard Mhacha, the Height of Macha).

The statue of Cúchulainn by the Irish artist Oliver Sheppard in the General Post Office, O'Connell Street, Dublin. Cúchulainn is the hero of the earlier of Ireland's two mythological cycles. Mortally wounded in his single-handed defence of Ulster against the forces of Queen Maeve of Connacht, he tied himself to a standing stone to maintain his defiance to the end. Only when at length a raven perched on his shoulder did his enemies dare approach. The statue symbolises the Easter Rising, 1916.

The round tower at Rattoo, County Kerry. Note the door raised above ground level for protection.

Dawn, Killary Harbour by Paul Henry (1876-1958). Born in Belfast, Henry, a distinguished landscape painter, was infatuated with Connemara, the unspoilt region of mountains, lakes, moorland, and coastal inlets west of Galway city—as have been innumerable artists since.

QUESTION 39

What famous Irish writer said on his deathbed, *"Does anybody understand?"*
Was it   (a) James Joyce?
         (b) Sir Richard Steele?
         (c) Joseph Sheridan Le Fanu?

QUESTION 40

Zozimus was a famous Dublin personality.
Was he   (a) a seventeenth-century seer?
         (b) an eighteenth-century physician who practised traditional
         medicine with remarkable success?
         (c) a nineteenth-century street reciter?

QUESTION 41

Historically, land ownership in Ireland has been at the core of social and economic affairs to an extent rarely experienced in other countries. At the end of the eighteenth century virtually all agricultural land was owned by about 5,000 land owners, the majority of whom differed (outside the areas of plantation in Ulster) in religion, language and national aspirations from their tenants, who had few rights and could generally be evicted at will. Following the repeal of the Corn Laws in 1846 and the devastation of the Famine of the 1840s, wholesale evictions became a feature of Irish rural life, culminating in the "Land War" of the 1870s and 1880s. One of the great national champions of the Irish tenantry was Charles Stewart Parnell, himself a landlord and a Protestant.

The outcome of the campaign for reform was a remarkable body of legislation, the Irish land code, which effected a bloodless social revolution of far-reaching consequences, whereby ownership of their holdings was transferred to 430,000 farming tenants in the Republic. (A parallel transfer of ownership was effected in Northern Ireland.) In addition, some two million acres were purchased by state agencies for redistribution among former tenants with uneconomic farms. This process, which began in a small way in 1881, received a major impetus with the "Balfour Act", called after the British prime minister, Arthur James Balfour (1848-1930), who subsequently lent his name to the "Balfour Declaration" of 1917 on a future national home for Jews in Palestine. When was the Irish Land Act known as the "Balfour Act" passed?
Was it in   (a) 1891?
         (b) 1901?
         (c) 1911?

ANSWER 39

(a) James Joyce (1882-1941). The publication of *Ulysses* in 1922 brought fame and comfort to Joyce. The following year he was at work on his vast experimental book of the night, *Finnegans Wake*. "Why", his wife Nora implored him, "don't you write sensible books that people can understand?" Joyce published the latter work, his "mess of mottage", in 1939 in the shadow of war, and fretted over the muted response of the literary critics. When war did come, Joyce fled Paris for Vichy and, later, Switzerland, where he died. He is buried in the Fluntern Cemetery in Zurich.

ANSWER 40

(c) a nineteenth-century street reciter. A native of the Liberties, Michael Moran (1794-1846) acquired the nickname "Zozimus" from a character in his most popular recitation. Although blind almost from birth, and of very deprived background, he was able to support himself and a family by the recitation of poems, songs and ballads, which he could recall on once hearing them. He is remembered mostly, however, for the following lines from his rendering of "The Finding of Moses":

> *On Egypt's banks, contagious to the Nile,*
> *The ould King Pharoah's daughter went to bathe in style;*
> *She took her dip, and came unto the land*
> *And for to dry her royal pelt she ran along the strand;*
> *A bulrush tripped her, whereupon she saw*
> *A smiling babby in a wad of straw;*
> *She took him up and says in accents mild,*
> *"Oh taranages, gerrls! which of yiz owns the child?"*

Dublin has always cherished its eccentrics, or "characters", at all levels of society. In more recent times these have included Pope O'Mahony, Johnny Forty-Coats and Bang-Bang (who boarded passing buses and "shot" the passengers with a key).

ANSWER 41

(a) 1891

QUESTION 42

What British poet wrote:

> For the great Gaels of Ireland
> Are the men that God made mad,
> For all their wars are merry,
> And all their songs are sad ?

Was it   (a) GK Chesterton (1874-1936)?
            (b) Alfred Lord Tennyson (1809-92)?
            (c) Rudyard Kipling (1865-1936)?

QUESTION 43

Anagram: The R O T B S E U L
A name for the unrest in Northern Ireland

QUESTION 44

A group of eminent Scandinavian designers, commissioned by the Irish government to report on design in Ireland, made the following observations in *Design in Ireland*: "*The Georgian tradition we regard as English, not Irish, in its origins, even if the considerable supply of Georgianism in Ireland is modified to give it some especial characteristics. In England, its natural home, it is barely alive and at the last extremity. This reminds us of a parallel with Denmark. Both Ireland and Denmark have a large overpowering neighbour, and as Ireland has been influenced by England, so Denmark has been influenced by Germany*". When was this seminal report, which revolutionised Irish industrial and commercial design standards, published?

Was it in   (a) 1952?
              (b) 1962?
              (c) 1972?

QUESTION 45

Which Irish writer said, "*He had been eight years upon a project for extracting sunbeams out of cucumbers, which were to be put into phials hermetically sealed, and let out to warm the air in raw inclement summers*"?

Was it   (a) Jonathan Swift in *Gulliver's Travels* ?
            (b) James Stephens in *The Crock of Gold* ?
            (c) Flann O'Brien in *The Dalkey Archive* ?

ANSWER 42

(a) GK Chesterton, in *The Ballad of the White Horse*. The Romans referred to the Irish as *Scotti* (Scots). A branch of the Irish Dál Riada tribe conquered Argyll at the end of the fifth century AD. By the end of the tenth century, the term *Scotti* was confined to their descendants in Britain and subsequently was used to name the land they held—Scotland. The Welsh called the Irish in Ireland *Gwyddyl*; the Irish adopted this name for themselves. Its modern form is "Gael". The name "Ireland" which was in use before the tenth century AD, is an English coinage, being a combination of "*Éire*" and "land".

ANSWER 43

Troubles. In the late 1960s the nationalist minority in Northern Ireland, inspired by the non-violent movement in America led by Martin Luther King, formed a Civil Rights movement aimed at removing discrimination against Catholics. Unfortunately the political structures in Northern Ireland could not cope democratically with such a movement. There were bloody repressive incidents, which revitalised the IRA. They began to attack British Army forces which had been despatched to Northern Ireland to protect nationalist communities from an extremist Protestant backlash against the Civil Rights movement. This in turn led to a spiral of violence involving the British Army, the IRA, and the Ulster Volunteer Force (UVF), an extremist Protestant paramilitary organisation. Neither the IRA nor the UVF represents the majority of the communities from which their members are drawn—in fact they have commanded only a relatively small proportion of the votes of their communities in elections whether in the North or South of Ireland.

ANSWER 44

(b) 1962

ANSWER 45

(a) Jonathan Swift in *Gulliver's Travels*. Ironically, Swift's great political satire became in time a classic children's story, and Gulliver entered the world's consciousness—a gentle giant pinned to the ground, as he slept, by the pygmy citizens of Lilliput. In 1897, the Dublin novelist Bram (for "Abraham") Stoker (1847-1912) published *Dracula* and also slipped into the world's consciousness the nightmarish figure of Count Dracula.

QUESTION 46

More people of Irish descent have the surname Murphy than any other—
certainly it is the most numerous surname in Ireland itself. Murphy's Law
states: "*If anything can go wrong, it will* ". Which Murphy formulated this law?
Was it   (a) Patrick V. Murphy, former New York Police Commissioner,
and subsequently director of the Police Foundation,
Washington?
(b) Francis Murphy (1890-1949), who studied law at Michigan
University, Lincoln's Inn, London and Trinity College
Dublin, and who was US attorney general from 1939 to
1940?
(c) Captain Ed Murphy, an engineer and pilot in the United
States Air Force?

QUESTION 47

Like most small economies the Irish economy is heavily dependent on foreign
trade in goods and services. Within the EU, only Belgium and Luxembourg are
more dependent on such trade. In the past, Ireland's overseas sales consisted
mainly of primary agricultural products. Since 1973, when Ireland joined the
EU, the volume of exports has grown steadily while the share of manufactured
goods in total exports has expanded form 45% to 77%. Three quarters of
Ireland's total sales abroad are to the EU; most of this trade is now to Ireland's
continental partners rather than the UK. Which of these buys the greatest
share?
Is it   (a) France?
(b) Germany?
(c) Italy?

QUESTION 48

Placenames in Ireland derive mostly from the Irish language, and generally
convey a meaning historical, religious, or descriptive. Both the English and
Irish versions are given on signposts in the Republic. The English versions
usually attempt a phonetic rendering of the Irish sounds. The longest
placename is descriptive of its location. It literally means "the soft place
between the two salt seas". In its English version how many letters does the
name contain?
Is it   (a) 22?
(b) 34?
(c) 42?

ANSWER 46

(c) Captain Ed Murphy, in 1949. This law has given rise to a host of subsidiary laws such as Murphy's Law of Thermodynamics ("Things get worse under pressure") and Murphy's Law of the Road ("Where there is a very long road with a narrow bridge, upon which there are two vehicles only, it follows that (a) the vehicles will be travelling in opposite directions, and (b) they will meet at the bridge"). Among the great number of behavioural laws and principles discovered since Murphy—by Parkinson, Peter and others—a significant number has been identified by people, like Murphy, with Irish surnames. Thus Duggan's Law states: "To every PhD there is an equal and opposite PhD" (this law explains why it is so easy to find expert witnesses who will contradict each other). Leahy's Law states: "If a thing is done wrong often enough, it becomes right".

ANSWER 47

(b) Germany with 13%. The UK with 32% is still Ireland's single largest customer. Ireland's exports of manufactured goods consist mainly of pharmaceutical products and computers. Because agriculture uses relatively little imported inputs, the value of agricultural exports to the net balance of payments is relatively very high. Tourism is the major component of the service industries. In 1992, visitors to Ireland spent £150,000,000 more than Irish visitors spent abroad.

ANSWER 48

(a) 22. Muckanaghederdauhaulia (in Irish *Muicneach idir dhá sháile*, also 22 letters) is near Costello (*casla*, "sea inlet") in Co. Galway. A knowledge of a few key components of the anglicisations of placenames will light the traveller's way considerably. Thus Bal-/Bally- (*baile*) indicates "town"/ "homestead"; Clon- (*cluain*) a "river meadow"; Drum- (*droim*) a "ridge of high ground"; Dun- (*dún*) a "stone fort"; Glen- (*gleann*) a "valley"; Inish-/Ennis- (*inis*) an "island"; Kill- (*cill*) a "church"; Lis(s)- (*lios*) and Rath- (*ráth*) a "prehistoric fort"; Slieve- (*sliabh*) a "mountain".

In Northern Ireland only the English versions are given on signposts. There is sometimes, among some of the Unionist population, antipathy to the Irish language and a general unawareness of the Gaelic origin of most of their placenames. When a suggestion was made to show both forms of the names in Co. Armagh in 1986, one of the county councillors proclaimed, "Over my dead body will they introduce a Gaelic name for Drumnahunsion!" Drumnahunsion means "the ridge of the ash tree" (*Droim na hUinseann*) in Irish. The splendid road atlas produced jointly in 1993 by the Ordnance Surveys in both parts of Ireland shows the two forms for all towns.

QUESTION 49

Beer was brewed from the waters of Babylon as far back as 2000 BC. The ancient Egyptians were partial to a drop and called it bouzah after the city of Bousiris on the Nile (whence, some say, "booze"). As far as beer-making in Ireland is concerned, the important date is 1759 when a young man, Arthur Guinness (1725-1803), founded a brewery at St James's Gate, one of the outer defences of the old walled city of Dublin. The brewery, which today occupies 25 hectares (62.5 acres) was at one time the largest in the world and is still the largest in Europe. It is the world's largest exporting brewery. It is also one of the most technologically advanced, capable of producing 2.5 million pints per day. Appropriately, the Guinness Worldwide Research Centre is located in Dublin. Today Guinness is brewed in 42 countries and sold in 140 from Abu Dhabi to Zambia. Over 10,000,000 glasses of the product are consumed every day throughout the world (two glasses make a pint, the traditional Irish measure). The Dublin beverage is produced from the same ingredients used by Arthur Guinness long ago—Irish-grown barley, hops, soft Dublin water, and even the same yeast strain introduced two hundred years ago. There are no chemicals or artificial additives of any kind. So far as the Guinness produced daily in other countries is concerned, they all contain a flavouring extract produced in Dublin from the original recipe. Incidentally, the drink came to be called "porter" because of its popularity with porters in the vegetable and fish markets of Covent Garden and Billingsgate in London.

The Guinness family have been generous patrons and benefactors of Dublin and Ireland, contributing to a wide variety of religious, educational, civic and cultural projects. What Dublin park, originally a neglected common, did Arthur Guinness (Lord Ardilaun) (1840-1915), grandson of the original Arthur, refurbish and present to the city of Dublin?

Was it (a) Merrion Square?
(b) St Stephen's Green?
(c) St Anne's Park?

QUESTION 50

Who wrote: *The harp that once through Tara's halls*
The soul of music shed,
Now hangs as mute on Tara's walls
As if that soul were fled ?

Was it (a) James Clarence Mangan?
(b) James Stephens?
(c) Thomas Moore?

QUESTION 51

Anagram (two words): H R I I B S T   E S S L I
Not a proper name for the west European archipelago?

ANSWER 49

(b) St Stephen's Green

ANSWER 50

(c) Thomas Moore (1779-1852) in his *Irish Melodies*. Tara, the ancient seat of the High Kings of Ireland, is in Co. Meath ("the Royal County"), an area of legendary lushness. Moore used the abandonment of Tara in the early Christian period as a symbol for the death of romantic Ireland. Tara gave its name to the O'Hara plantation in *Gone with the Wind*.

Moore, who was born in Dublin, was a friend of Byron and Shelley. His *Irish Melodies* contains his best-known lyrics, "The Last Rose of Summer" and "Oft in the Stilly Night". In 1817 he published *Lalla Rookh*, a narrative poem with an exotic Oriental setting which became probably the most translated poem of its time, and earned Moore the highest price paid up till then by a publisher for a poem in English (£3,000). The poem also won Moore a reputation rivalling that of Byron and Scott. Moore's statue stands in College Green, Dublin, facing the colonnaded splendour of the Bank of Ireland.

ANSWER 51

British Isles. The first use of the term "The British Isles" occurs in Heylin's *Microcosmus* (1621) as a page heading. The general practice of cartographers had been to name Ireland in its own right. The use of "Britain" and "British" as modern political terms originated in the imperialism of Tudor England— "Britain" was the term favoured for the union of England and Wales (its use flattered the Welsh who were the last of the Britanni, the original Celtic inhabitants of Britain). When James VI of Scotland became James I of England in 1604, he was also proclaimed "King of Great Britain" (that term originally differentiated the island from the duchy of Brittany in France, known as "Little Britain"). After 1707, when Scotland was brought within the jurisdiction of the Westminster parliament, acts of parliament often referred to England and Scotland as South Britain and North Britain. Following the Act of Union in 1800 and the suppression of the Irish parliament, Ireland was sometimes referred to as West Britain (that term, in the form "West Briton", survived as a derogatory expression used by Irish nationalists for an Irish person who was a British sympathiser).

Because it is a vestige of English imperialism, the term "British Isles" is offensive to many Irish people, and of course it is not used in the historic Downing Street Declaration of 1993. The growing understanding and warmth in relations between the people of Ireland and Britain is likely in time to lead to its total discontinuance. The terms "Ireland and Britain", "Britain and Ireland" or "these islands" serve most contexts adequately.

QUESTION 52

Anagram: N I B N O S R O
The name of Ireland's president

QUESTION 53

During the second half of the nineteenth century Germany succeeded in breaking Britain's dominance of the iron and steel market. What Irish engineer played a leading role in that endeavour?

Was it   (a) William Dargan (1799-1867), who constructed the first railway in Ireland (Dublin to Kingstown, now Dún Laoghaire) on which the inaugural journey was made on 14 December 1834?

(b) William Thomas Mulvany (1806-1885), the first person to attempt the drainage of the Shannon?

(c) Richard Griffith (1784-1878), who carried out the great Valuation of Rateable Property in Ireland?

QUESTION 54

What Irishman—and former European Commissioner—became in 1993 director general of the world trade body, the General Agreement on Tariffs and Trade (GATT), based in Geneva?

Was it   (a) Peter Sutherland?

(b) Patrick J. Hillery?

(c) Ray MacSharry?

QUESTION 55

George Bernard Shaw, who reputedly once wrote to a friend, "I have written you a long letter because I haven't time to write a short one", was born in Synge Street, Dublin. A statue of Shaw stands outside one of Dublin's public buildings.

Is it   (a) Trinity College?

(b) The National Gallery of Ireland?

(c) The Abbey Theatre?

QUESTION 56

In 1991, the percentage of the population under 15 was 16.2 in Germany, 19.4 in Spain, 20.1 in France and 20.9 in Portugal. What was it in Ireland?

Was it   (a) 25.9?

(b) 26.9?

(c) 27.9?

ANSWER 52

Robinson. When she was elected in 1990, Mrs Mary Robinson became the seventh President of Ireland and the first woman president. Of the 183 states at that time, only six had women as monarchs or elected presidents – Denmark, Iceland, the Netherlands, Nicaragua, the Philippines and the United Kingdom. In addition, two Commonwealth states had women as governors general—Belize and New Zealand. Under the constitution of Ireland, the office of president is largely ceremonial.

ANSWER 53

(b) William Thomas Mulvany. Born in Sandymount, Dublin, Mulvany spent his early career in the Board of Works. He was retired early when he ran foul of that most powerful of pressure groups in nineteenth century Ireland—the landed gentry. In 1853 Mulvany accepted the invitation of a fellow-Irishman, Michael Corr, who had property in the Ruhr, to establish and manage a mining company in Germany. The Hibernia, opened on St Patrick's Day 1856, became one of the great mines of the Ruhr and survived until 1967. Mulvany extended his interests to iron-smelting. When he had consolidated his businesses, he became deeply involved in the politics of German economic development (in contrast to Alfred Krupp, the steel-manufacturer and August Thyssen, the iron smelter, who concentrated on creating their own industrial empires). As director of the German Iron and Steel Industrialists' Society, Mulvany master-minded German competition with Britain. In 1881, the twenty-fifth anniversary of the opening of the Hibernia mine, Mulvany was hailed as the Grand Old Man of German industry—the King of Prussia awarded him a gold medal, congratulatory addresses were presented to him, and he was made a freeman of a number of cities. He died in Dusseldorf.

ANSWER 54

(a) Peter Sutherland

ANSWER 55

(b) The National Gallery of Ireland. In his will, Shaw left one-third of a large trust fund to the gallery. This has been used to acquire paintings and generally enhance the building in Merrion Square. Royalties from Shaw's works and in particular from *My Fair Lady*, which is based on Shaw's *Pygmalion*, have substantially enlarged the fund.

ANSWER 56

(b) 26.9, the highest in the EU

QUESTION 57

The population of Australia is seventeen million. How many are of Irish extraction?

Is it   (a) one million?
        (b) three million?
        (c) five million?

QUESTION 58

Anagram: Y E F I L F
The river Dublin is built on

QUESTION 59

In 1940 the Irish government headed by Éamon de Valera established the Dublin Institute for Advanced Studies. A number of distinguished physicists from Eastern Europe (whose philosophical outlook differed profoundly from that of the masses of the Irish people) were afforded a refuge and a livelihood there at the outbreak of World War II. Within a few years, scholars from the Institute's School of Celtic Studies became embroiled in a heated controversy over whether there was one St Patrick or two. An Irish writer subsequently observed that it was the singular achievement of the Dublin Institute for Advanced Studies to prove there were two St Patricks and no God.

Was he   (a) Myles na gCopaleen (Brian O'Nolan, alias Flann O'Brien)?
        (b) Brendan Behan?
        (c) Seán Ó Faoláin?

QUESTION 60

The Shannon, which rises in Co. Cavan and flows 372 km to the Atlantic Ocean beyond Limerick, is the longest river in Ireland and Britain. It is almost as long as which of the following:

        (a) the Ebro?
        (b) the Loire?
        (c) the Tiber?

QUESTION 61

Anagram: T E A N O
Well known in Toronto

ANSWER 57

(c) five million, almost one third of the total—a larger proportion of people of Irish extraction than in the USA. About a quarter of the immigrants into Australia from its foundation as a British colony in 1788 down to the early decades of the twentieth century came from Ireland. (Since 1914, Irish emigration to Australia has been relatively small.) About one in ten of these was a convict (and many of those were transported political prisoners). While Irish emigrants to the USA in the nineteenth century settled mainly in the major cities (they had neither the skills nor the capital to set up in farming), those to Australia, a vast, empty continent, contributed their due part to agriculture, Australia's biggest single industry. They were mostly to be found on small, mixed farms; but there were almost as many Irish as Scottish great station owners.

Eighty to eighty-five per cent of Irish emigrants to Australia were Catholics and they became particularly prominent in politics, law, journalism, and education. But the fifteen to twenty per cent of Irish emigrants who were Protestants contributed to the rich weave of Australia's cultural life, too, through a host of distinguished judges, bishops, publicists and professors, mainly from Trinity College Dublin, and a stream of Ulster Presbyterians, who worked mostly in small farming communities.

ANSWER 58

Liffey—Joyce's "Anna Livia Plurabelle"

ANSWER 59

(a) Myles na gCopaleen

ANSWER 60

(c) the Tiber, which flows 405 km from the Apennines to the sea beyond Rome. The Ebro is 910 km long and the Loire 1,020 km.

ANSWER 61

Eaton. Timothy Eaton (1834-1907) was born near Ballymena, Co. Antrim. He emigrated to Canada and established a successful retail business, which has developed into Toronto's Eaton Centre, one of the world's leading shopping and commercial complexes.

QUESTION 62

Anagram: B U N D L I
A capital place!

QUESTION 63

> *Ich am of Irlaunde,*
> *And of the holy londe*
> *Of Irlaunde.*
>
> *Gode sire, pray ich thee,*
> *For of sainte charitee,*
> *Come and daunce wit me*
> *In Irlaunde.*

This fragment from an English source, possibly the earliest poem in English about Ireland, may have been part of a *carole*, a ring-dance with song in which the dancers circled hand in hand while they sang the refrain and danced on the spot while they sang the stanzas. (The word "stanza" is Italian—it originally meant a stopping place—and derives from the Latin *stare*, to stand.) When were the lines written?

Was it in   (a) the late twelfth century?
           (b) the early fourteenth century?
           (c) the mid-sixteenth century?

QUESTION 64

For elections, Ireland, like most EU countries, uses a proportional representation (PR) system, however by means of a single transferable vote rather than a list system. When was PR introduced to Ireland?

Was it in   (a) 1919?
           (b) 1929?
           (c) 1939?

QUESTION 65

Who said, "*Happiness is no laughing matter*"?

Was it   (a) Oliver Goldsmith?
        (b) Brendan Behan?
        (c) Archbishop Whately of Dublin?

ANSWER 62

Dublin. Founded over a thousand years ago, Ireland's capital has a population of one million, taking into account both the city and its built-up environs. Dublin is beautifully sited "by bend of bay and swerve of shore" as Joyce has it in *Finnegans Wake*. Through it flow "the hitherandthithering waters" of the Liffey. Behind it, the mountains hold themselves apart in dark, deep-wooded contemplation. Dublin has a substantial inheritance in stone from various periods—cathedrals, theatres, universities, banks, shops, public buildings. Down by the quays is the splendid two-hundred-year-old Custom House, possibly the finest building in Ireland. Dublin presents predominantly as a Georgian (1714-1830) and Victorian (1837-1901) city, and indeed its exceptional Georgian squares are among Europe's architectural treasures. A great literary city, Dublin has a vibrant and distinctive pub culture in which whimsy and reality mix their thinks.

ANSWER 63

(b) the early fourteenth century. *Ich am* means "I am" in Chaucerian English.

ANSWER 64

(a) 1919, for an election to Sligo corporation. PR was embodied in the Constitution of the Irish Free State 1922 and subsequently in *Bunreacht na hÉireann* (the Constitution of Ireland) 1937. The acronym PR usually refers to public relations, a profession pioneered by the American Ivy Lee in the early years of the twentieth century. Ireland's Electricity Supply Board was the first organisation in Europe to appoint a public relations officer—it did so in 1927 to promote the Shannon Scheme. The UK's Empire Marketing Board was the second.

ANSWER 65

(c) Archbishop Whately (1783-1863), in *Apothegms*. Whately, a leading Anglican, was responsible for the inclusion in Irish school-texts of the verses from *Hymns for Infant Minds* by Anne and Jane Taylor, which have never been forgiven him:

> *I thank the goodness and the grace*
> *Which on my birth have smiled,*
> *And made me, in these Christian days,*
> *A happy English child.*

During the nineteenth century the English authorities in Ireland attempted a programme of anglicisation comparable to the Czar's Russification programme.

International rugby match, Scotland v Ireland. Ireland's first rugby international was against England in London in 1875 (England won).

Jack Charlton, manager of the Republic of Ireland soccer team since 1986. Under his regime the team reached the finals of the World Cup for the first time in 1990 and for the second time in 1994. The most popular Englishman in Ireland.

Dawson Stelfox. In 1993 the Belfastman became the first Irishman to climb Mount Everest. In 1921, an Irishman, CK Howard Bury from Mullingar, led the first British reconnaissance trip to the approaches of Mount Everest.

Sonia O'Sullivan from Cork is one of the fastest runners in the world. She won the silver medal in the women's world 1500 metres race at Stuttgart in 1993.

41

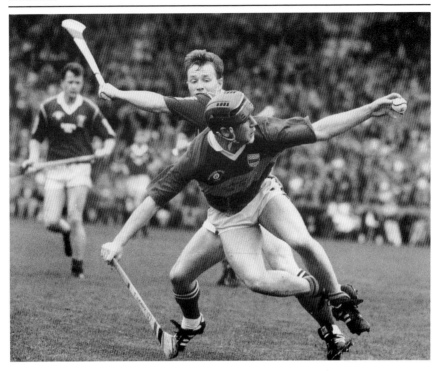

The clash of the ash. Hurling, which is played with sticks worked from the ash tree and a leather ball, is Ireland's oldest field game and one of the fastest in the world.

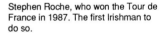

Stephen Roche, who won the Tour de France in 1987. The first Irishman to do so.

The Irish Derby, worth IR£600,000 in prize money, is one of the most prestigious races in the world. It is held at the Curragh in August after the English and French Derbies, whose winners it usually attracts. The Irish thoroughbred industry earns IR£60 million in exports (of about 4,000 horses) each year.

QUESTION 66

Who said, *"Ulster at the proper moment will resort to its supreme arbitrament of force. Ulster will fight; Ulster will be right"*?

Was it   (a) Edward Henry Carson (1845-1935), the Dublin-born barrister and leader of the Ulster Unionists?

(b) James Craig (1871-1940), the first Prime Minister of Northern Ireland?

(c) Lord Randolph Churchill (1849-94), the British Conservative?

QUESTION 67

Anagram: S L P O I I C T
You find this in every state

QUESTION 68

There were three German-speaking communities in Ireland in the eighteenth century: Moravians at Gracehill, Co. Antrim, Lutherans in Dublin, and Palatines in Co. Limerick. The Palatines were by far the largest group, being descended from 800 families brought to Ireland by Queen Anne in 1709 "to strengthen the Protestant interest". They settled mainly in Co. Limerick. They maintained their own burgomaster and German language until the early nineteenth century. One of their claims to fame is that they introduced into Ireland the practice of sowing potatoes in drills. Their descendants, long since assimilated into the Methodist, Church of Ireland and Roman Catholic communities around them, are still numerous in the areas where they settled, and many of their surnames survive, such as Bovenizer, Heavenor, Shoemaker (Schumacher), Switzer. The Palatines were so called because they came from the Palatinate, a region in south-west Germany once ruled by counts palatine, that is, counts entitled to exercise royal prerogatives in their territories. What county in Ireland once constituted a palatinate?

Was it   (a) Meath?

(b) Kilkenny?

(c) Waterford?

QUESTION 69

According to the US Census Bureau, is the Irish ethnic group in the US at forty million

(a) the third largest?

(b) the fifth largest?

(c) the seventh largest?

ANSWER 66

(c) Lord Randolph Churchill, Winston Churchill's father. At the end of the nineteenth century the ruling Liberal Party at Westminster was prepared to give Home Rule (a limited form of self-government) to Ireland. The Ulster Unionists, for whom Home Rule was Rome Rule, i.e. rule by the Roman Catholic Church, were intent on resisting its imposition, by force if necessary. The Tories, of whom Lord Churchill was a leader, in order to bring down the Liberals, were prepared "to play the Orange card", that is, to support the Unionists' resort to force.

ANSWER 67

politics. In the Republic there are (1994) six political parties represented in the Dáil. The two largest, Fianna Fáil and Fine Gael, were formed out of the split in Sinn Féin, the great national movement, caused by the rejection of the Anglo-Irish Treaty of 1922 by a substantial minority of the Dáil. Since they aim to be broadly-based national parties, Fianna Fáil and Fine Gael occupy the political centre, swaying pragmatically to left or right. The other four parties, the Labour Party, the Progressive Democrats, the Democratic Left and the Green Party, together command 53 of the 166 seats in the Dáil. In Northern Ireland there are five major parties. The Unionist majority is represented by the Ulster Unionist Party (UUP) and the Democratic Unionist Party (DUP). The Nationalists are represented by the Social Democratic and Labour Party (SDLP) and Sinn Féin. (A remnant of the original Sinn Féin who refused to recognise the constitutional arrangements accepted by the majority of the people retained the name Sinn Féin.) The Alliance Party attracts support from both traditions in Northern Ireland.

ANSWER 68

(b) Kilkenny, under the Dukes of Ormonde

ANSWER 69

(a) the third largest, behind the English and German groups with fifty million each. African-Americans number thirty million, Hispanics eighteen million, French thirteen million, Italians twelve million, Scots ten million. American Indians number only one-and-a-half million.

QUESTION 70

What Irish writer said, *"Woman begins by resisting a man's advances and ends by blocking his retreat "*?

      Was it   (a) George Bernard Shaw in *Man and Superman* ?

               (b) Oliver St John Gogarty in *As I was Going Down Sackville Street* ?

               (c) Oscar Wilde in *An Ideal Husband* ?

QUESTION 71

Anagram: N I L I K A
The bishopric of Würzburg in Germany is named in honour of this seventh-century Irish saint, and hundreds of churches all over Germany are dedicated to him. In Dublin the German School bears his name.

QUESTION 72

Ireland is ideal for horses: they thrive in its moderate climate, which provides them with plentiful pasturage, and the limestone soil, rich in calcium, promotes strong bones. The natural focus of the Irish horse industry is the Curragh of Kildare, where horses have been raced for two thousand years (the Irish word curragh means "racecourse"). The Normans introduced the Norman Great Horse (a powerful animal favoured by the crusaders), which was interbred with the native breed, a smaller animal. The result, the Irish Draught, was a lighter and faster animal much sought after as a cavalry horse in Ireland and abroad. Today, the Irish Draught, when crossed with a thoroughbred, produces another much sought-after animal, the Irish Show Jumper. Another Irish breed, the Connemara Pony, is descended from the small native Irish horses which were crossed with Spanish Barbs and Andalucian horses imported into Galway as part of the trade between that city and Spain down to the seventeenth century.

    The first steeplechase ever recorded took place, as a result of a wager in 1752, from the church at Buttevant, Co. Cork, to the church of St Leger, whose steeple (hence the name) could be seen four miles away. (The name Buttevant derives from the French *Boutez-en-avant*, "Press on ahead!", the war-cry of the Norman de Barrys.) Notwithstanding the advent of mechanised agriculture, which has virtually eliminated the horse as a farm animal, there are still 50,000 horses in the Republic. Many of these are bloodstock, all of which must be recorded in the national stud book. All thoroughbreds throughout the world trace their descent to at least one of three Arab horses imported into Britain at the end of the seventeenth or beginning of the eighteenth century. One of these saw action at the Battle of the Boyne in 1690.

      Was it   (a) The Byerly Turk?

               (b) The Godolphin Barb?

               (c) The Darley Arabian?

ANSWER 70

(c) Oscar Wilde in *An Ideal Husband*. Gogarty, a less famous writer than the other two, was a successful surgeon and well-known wit. In his poem "Leda and the Swan", based on Ovid's account of how Zeus, the sportive chief of the Greek gods, transformed himself into a swan the better to ravish the lovely Leda, Gogarty describes Leda's mother's reaction when Leda tells her she's pregnant:

> *Of the tales that daughters*
> *Tell their poor old mothers,*
> *Which by all accounts are*
> *Often very odd;*
> *Leda's was a story*
> *Stranger than all others.*
> *What was there to say but:*
> *Glory be to God?*

Gogarty appears in the opening sentence of James Joyce's *Ulysses* as "Stately, plump Buck Mulligan..."

ANSWER 71

Kilian. In Celtic Ireland, the native legal code, the Brehon laws, did not provide for capital punishment, so one of the severest punishments was exile. Irish monks, therefore, felt they could show their love of Christ in no greater way than by going abroad as missionaries. Because Irish monasteries were centres of learning, wherever the monks brought Christianity they brought learning too (hence the description of Ireland during the Dark Ages as *insula sanctorum et doctorum*, "the island of saints and scholars"; the phrase *insula sanctorum* is first found in an eleventh-century manuscript). Kilian set up his headquarters in Würzburg, the capital of the province of Franconia. He and his companions proceeded to convert the whole province to Christianity. Kilian fell foul of the ruler's wife, who arranged for his murder and that of his two companions. In 1989 the Irish and German postal authorities jointly issued a stamp to commemorate the 1,300th anniversary of their martyrdom.

ANSWER 72

(a) The Byerly Turk, ridden by a Williamite officer, Captain Byerly

QUESTION 73

Bernardo O'Higgins (1778-1842), whose father came from Co. Meath, was one of the leading figures in the successful revolt of a Latin American country against Spanish colonial rule; he became first president of the new republic (1818-23). What is the name of the country?

Is it   (a) Bolivia?
         (b) Peru?
         (c) Chile?

QUESTION 74

Anagram: C A N N Y C A S E D
A class of an Irishman

QUESTION 75

The Giant's Causeway is a spectacular natural phenomenon consisting of a promontory of regular polygonal basalt columns which extends for half a kilometre from the northern coast of Co. Antrim. Strictly speaking, it should be the Giants' Causeway, since it is named after the Fomorians, a fearsome race of giants in Irish mythology. How many sides have the columns which constitute the Causeway?

Do they have (a) five sides?
            (b) six sides?
            (c) nine sides?

QUESTION 76

Which Irishman said, "*Experience is the name everyone gives to their mistakes* "?

Was it   (a) Oscar Wilde?
         (b) Conor Cruise O'Brien?
         (c) Edmund Burke?

QUESTION 77

The biggest crowd ever to assemble in Ireland—over a million people—greeted Pope John Paul II in the Phoenix Park, Dublin, when he paid the first visit by a Roman Pontiff to Ireland. What year was that?

Was it   (a) 1979?
         (b) 1980?
         (c) 1981?

ANSWER 73

(c) Chile

ANSWER 74

Ascendancy. The Ascendancy is the name given to the propertied class in Ireland which was loyal to the English Crown from the Battle of the Boyne (1690) until the land reforms at the end of the nineteenth century, which swept away the last of their political power. The Ascendancy consisted of a small class who had benefited from a series of land confiscations from Catholic land owners. Their heyday was the eighteenth century, when about 5,000 of them owned 95% of the land of Ireland. Associated with them were the professional classes. It was possible for Catholics to join them, provided they conformed to the Protestant faith, and some did, like the forebears of Arthur Guinness, founder of Guinness's Brewery; Speaker William Conolly of the Irish parliament, reputed to be the wealthiest man in Ireland in his day (his magnificent residence outside Dublin, Castletown House, is open to visitors); and the father of John Fitzgibbon, later Lord Clare, architect of the Act of Union (1800). Some members of this class became patrons of the arts and sciences, and to them Dublin owes its fine Georgian buildings and its broad streets. From this class, too, came many of Ireland's greatest patriots, such as Henry Grattan, Robert Emmet, and Lord Edward Fitzgerald. Douglas Hyde, the first President of Ireland (1938-45), came from the same background.

ANSWER 75

All three. There is also one column with eight sides (known as the Key-stone), and one with three.

ANSWER 76

(a) Oscar Wilde in *Lady Windermere's Fan*. Conor Cruise O'Brien (1917-), historian, diplomat, UN representative in Katanga, government minister, university rector, critic, newspaper editor and playwright, is probably the most famous of Ireland's contemporary intellectuals. His literary masterpiece is *The Great Melody* (1992), a biography of Edmund Burke.

ANSWER 77

(a) 1979

QUESTION 78

What famous European psychologist said, *"The Irish are the only race which can't be psycho-analysed; they're too ready to invent dreams or to contrive lies more interesting than the truth"*?

Was it   (a) Alfred Adler (1870-1937), born in Austria?
           (b) Sigmund Freud (1856-1939), also born in Austria?
           (c) Carl Gustav Jung (1875-1961), born in Switzerland?

QUESTION 79

In 1926 Éamon de Valera, the leader of the anti-Treaty republicans who were defeated in the civil war, founded a new political party, Fianna Fáil ("The Soldiers of Destiny"). The party entered the Dáil in 1927, and gained power in 1932. It has remained the dominant party in Irish politics ever since. De Valera drew up a new constitution, Bunreacht na hÉireann in Irish, which replaced that of the Irish Free State adopted following the Anglo-Irish Treaty of 1921. The new constitution was enacted by the people in a referendum. In which year was the referendum held?

Was it in: (a) 1935?
           (b) 1937?
           (c) 1939?

QUESTION 80

This 1934 classic documentary film, unparalleled in its time for visual imagery, and made by the Irish-American director Robert Flaherty, chronicles the struggle of islanders off the west coast of Ireland to wrest a living from the Atlantic.
What is the missing word?

Man of _____

QUESTION 81

St Patrick (died *c.*490), the patron saint of Ireland, was not himself an Irishman. Where was he born?

Was it in   (a) Wales?
           (b) Scotland?
           (c) France?

QUESTION 82

Anagram: I M P G O N Y A L
A play by George Bernard Shaw

ANSWER 78

(b) Sigmund Freud, as quoted by Anthony Burgess (1917-93) in *The Observer*. Burgess, the prolific author of *A Clockwork Orange, Here Comes Everybody—an introduction to James Joyce* and *Earthly Powers,* was born in Manchester. His background was predominantly Irish.

ANSWER 79

(b) 1937. Fianna Fáil is derived from two Irish words. The Fianna were a group of heroes led by Fionn Mac Cool. They were believed to be a standing army in the service of the High King Cormac Mac Airt, who flourished in the third century AD. *Fál* is an Irish word meaning "destiny". The Lia Fáil (the Stone of Destiny) is a famous stone on the Hill of Tara in Co. Meath at which the pagan High Kings stood at their inauguration. The name of another major political party, Fine Gael, also derives from two Irish words. *Fine* means "extended family". *Gael* means "Irish".

ANSWER 80

Aran

ANSWER 81

(a) Wales is the most likely answer. Patrick spent six years of his youth as a slave in Ireland. He himself tells us in his *Confession,* written in Latin, that he was born at *Bannaven Taburniae,* a placename which does not occur in any other Latin records. This could be Patrick's phonetic rendering in Latin of a place known to the Irish, whose language was still unwritten, as *"Bun Abhann tSabhrainne",* literally Severn Mouth. That part of the British coastline would have been the most vulnerable to the Irish freebooters who captured Patrick.

ANSWER 82

Pygmalion. The story is told of a French student in London struggling hard to master spoken English who, the day following the première of *Pygmalion,* was exasperated to read a newspaper headline: PYGMALION PRONOUNCED SUCCESS.

Shaw's plays attracted the interest of Hollywood's moguls but Shaw was averse to having his work reshaped by their box office values. When Sam Goldwyn visited Shaw in 1920, he assured the distinguished author he would treat his plays with velvet gloves, that their integrity would be preserved, commercial considerations be damned. Later, Shaw told a newspaperman, anxious to know how the meeting between the famous Irishman and the famous Jew had gone, "There is only one difference between Mr Goldwyn and me. Whereas he is after art I am after money". Both Goldwyn and Shaw dined out on the witticism for years.

QUESTION 83

Who said, *"Proper words in proper places make the true definition of style"*?
>Was it (a) John Millington Synge?
>(b) Jonathan Swift?
>(c) James Joyce?

QUESTION 84

The Irish have been in Newfoundland since the early eighteenth century at least, when Bristol fishing vessels habitually stopped at Waterford to take on provisions, crew members and workers for the Newfoundland fisheries. (As a result, Newfoundland is called Talamh an Éisc – "Land of Fish" – in Irish.) By the 1850s over half a million Irish had emigrated to British North America. Today their descendants number 10% of the population. A significant number of these are of Ulster Protestant origin. Initially, the Irish Catholics were often at odds with their French-speaking co-religionists on linguistic grounds, and with the Protestant English-speaking majority because their loyalty was considered doubtful. The situation was not alleviated by the five Fenian incursions into Canada from the United States between 1866 and 1870, nor by the assassination (believed to have been carried out by a Fenian), in 1868, of Thomas D'Arcy McGee, the former Young Irelander who had become a leading Canadian statesman. Today, the Catholic Irish have fully integrated into Canadian life.

Of which Irishman was it said, *"As an articulate but feisty leader of Irish Catholics, he provided an important mechanism for accommodating that group within Canadian society"*?
>Was it (a) Sir George Arthur French (1841-1921), born at Frenchpark, Co. Roscommon, and first commissioner of the North-West Mounted Police?
>(b) Timothy Warren Anglim (1822-96), born at Clonakilty, Co. Cork, MP for Ottawa from 1867 to 1882 and Speaker of the House of Commons from 1873 to 1878?
>(c) Daniel John O'Donovan (1844-1907), born at Killarney, Co. Kerry, who has been described as the father of the Canadian Labour movement, and who was Canada's first fair wages officer from 1900 to 1907?

QUESTION 85

Anagram: E H A T A C S I O
Ireland's prime minister

QUESTION 86

One of the largest voluntary childcare services in the world was established by an Irishman.
>Was it (a) The Society for the Prevention of Cruelty to Children?
>(b) The Save the Children Fund?
>(c) Barnardo's?

ANSWER 83

(b) Jonathan Swift (1667-1745), in *Letter to a Young Clergyman*. In his *Lives of the Poets*, Samuel Johnson wrote of Swift, who was born in Dublin and educated in Kilkenny and Trinity College, Dublin, "It was said...that Swift had never been known to take a single thought from any writer, ancient or modern. This is not literally true; but perhaps no writer can easily be found that has borrowed so little, or that in all his excellences and all his defects has so well maintained his claim to be considered as original".

ANSWER 84

(b) Timothy Warren Anglim. The remark was made by his biographer, William M. Baker.

ANSWER 85

Taoiseach. The 1937 Constitution of Ireland introduced the term "Taoiseach", pronounced almost like "tee-shock", for the prime minister of Ireland. "Taoiseach" means "chief" in Irish. People who know no Irish may be surprised to learn that a form of the word "taoiseach" lurks in the commonplace term "macintosh". Charles Macintosh (1760-1843) was the eponymous Scottish chemist who patented the weatherproof overcoat; his surname was an anglicisation of the Scots Gaelic "Mac an Tòisich"—"the son of the chief". The Taoiseach, the state's chief executive, heads a cabinet government on the Westminster model. Ireland's head of state is the President.

ANSWER 86

(c) Barnardo's. Various humanitarian reformers in Victorian Britain such as Lord Shaftesbury campaigned tirelessly for the protection of children. By far the most colourful and controversial of those was Thomas Barnardo (1845-1905), a zealous evangelist. Barnardo was an Irishman who left his native Dublin in 1866 (the family name still appears on a furrier's shop in Dublin's Grafton Street) to train as a doctor so that he could bring medicine and Christianity to the Chinese. But he was so appalled by the child poverty of London that he remained there for the rest of his life. He set about establishing homes which, in time, have spread to every town of significance in Britain. It was said of Barnardo that he practically invented the waif. With his sense of showmanship and journalistic flair he dramatised their misery in endless publications and aroused an extraordinary interest in their welfare. He was a pioneer of street rescue, walking the slums at night, lantern in hand and with cakes in his pockets, "catching" destitute children. While many criticisms could be made of the early Barnardo organisation, it has developed into an enlightened professional childcare service. Ireland has an independent Barnardo organisation providing a range of services for children and families needing support in the Dublin area as well as serving on a national basis as a source of expert advice and guidance on childcare matters.

QUESTION 87

Anagram: B R Y N L E A
Don't believe a word of it!

QUESTION 88

What member of the Irish Ascendancy class said, *"Damn posterity, sir! What has posterity ever done for us?"*

Was it   (a) "Buck" Whaley (1766-1800), who walked from Dublin to Jerusalem and back within a year to win a wager of £20,000?

(b) Alfred Harmsworth Viscount Northcliffe (1865-1922), born in Chapelizod, Dublin, who created a publishing and newspaper empire by seizing on the readership potential created by the British Education Act of 1870, which greatly extended literacy?

(c) Sir Boyle Roche (1743-1807), politician and supporter of the Act of Union between Ireland and Britain in 1800?

QUESTION 89

The father of Henry Ford (1863-1947), the pioneer automobile manufacturer (by 1915 the Ford Motor Company was the world's largest car producer), was born in Ireland.
Did he come from:

(a) Co. Dublin?
(b) Co. Cork?
(c) Co. Waterford?

QUESTION 90

The population of Ireland is the result of the intermingling of many peoples throughout the ages. However, some widely distributed characteristics can be observed. Over half the population belongs to blood group O (indicating a Nordic strain); about half has blue eyes and a huge majority has brown hair. What percentage has red hair, often associated with fieriness—and Irishness?

Is it   (a) 4%?
(b) 6%?
(c) 8%?

ANSWER 87

blarney. "Blarney" means honeyed words meant to deceive. It is said to have come into the English language this way. Blarney is a village 8 km north-west of Cork city. During the time of Queen Elizabeth I the castle of Blarney, the strongest castle in Munster, with walls 6 metres thick, was held by Cormac MacCarthy, Lord of Muskerry. He found himself, as other Irish chieftains did, under intense pressure to renounce the Gaelic system by which he held his titles and privileges and to accept tenure of his lands from the English crown. MacCarthy gave the impression that he would concur, but from day to day put off doing anything about it "with fair words and soft speech". Finally, Elizabeth became exasperated. "This is all Blarney!" she declared. "What he says he never means". Blarney is famous today for the Blarney Stone, which traditionally has the power to confer eloquence on all those who kiss it.

English borrows quite a number of colourful words from Irish. The following are some examples: "banshee", a female spectral harbinger of death (it literally means "a fairy woman"); "galore", from the Irish *go leor,* means "aplenty"; "slogan" derives from the Irish *sluaghairm* "a war cry"; and "slew", as in "a slew of troubles" comes from the Irish *slua* "a crowd", "a host".

ANSWER 88

(c) Sir Boyle Roche, the classic exponent of the Irish bull, which the dictionary defines as an expression containing a manifest contradiction in terms unperceived by a speaker. Thus, defending his support for the British government in its policy towards Ireland, for which he received handsome financial rewards, he said that his love for both Ireland and England was such that he "would have the two sisters embrace like one brother". In a letter to a friend in England Boyle Roche sought to convey the parlous security situation in Ireland: "I write this with a sword in one hand and a pistol in the other".

ANSWER 89

(b) Co. Cork (Ballinascarthy), hence the long association of Cork city with the Ford Motor Company which in 1917 established a factory there for the production of Fordson tractors for the Russian market ("There was, it was true, some personal sentiment in it", said Ford, who visited Cork in 1912 to choose the site for the factory). Ford cars were assembled in Cork up to 1984. Since then Ford have maintained Cork as the centre for the distribution of Ford products in Ireland. Incidentally, Americans of Irish descent are now a leading group in corporate America.

ANSWER 90

(a) 4%

QUESTION 91

Anagram: S T O O R A T E N E C
A kind of shrub

QUESTION 92

What famous nineteenth-century French writer said, *"Four men [in this century] will have had a magnificent life: Napoleon, Cuvier and O'Connell, and I wish to be the fourth"*?

Was it   (a) Emile Zola (1840-1902)?
              (b) Honoré de Balzac (1799-1850)?
              (c) Victor Marie Hugo (1802-85)?

QUESTION 93

The Irish National Stud, open to the public, is located at Tully near the town of Kildare. The stud contains an equestrian museum which presents the history of the horse. Among the exhibits is the skeleton of the famous Tulyar. In the grounds are the Japanese Gardens, which are laid out to trace the life of man, by means of garden features, from the arrival of the soul on earth through the Gate of Oblivion, and thence along many paths and adventures such as the tunnel of childhood ignorance, the adolescent hill of learning and the parting of the ways, where the young person must choose between a single state and marriage. The traveller taking the latter path reaches an island symbolising the joy and wonder of courtship, crosses the engagement and the marriage bridges and traverses the honeymoon path. The way of life is attended by joys, hazards, disappointments and pitfalls, but leads to the hill of ambition from which the traveller can look back on his or her past life before descending to the well of wisdom and the chair of old age, finally leaving the garden through the Gateway to Eternity. The gardens are laid out in an authentic Japanese style, and contain Japanese flowers, shrubs and trees. In which century were the gardens laid out?

Was it the   (a) eighteenth?
               (b) nineteenth?
               (c) twentieth?

QUESTION 94

Karl Marx and Friedrich Engels published *The Communist Manifesto* in 1848. Engels (1820-95) married an Irishwoman, Lizzie Burns, and visited Ireland twice. He learned Irish in order to spread the Marxist doctrine in Ireland. However, the *Manifesto* was not published in Irish until which of the following dates:

               (a) 1890?
               (b) 1913?
               (c) 1986?

ANSWER 91

cotoneaster. Augustine Henry (1857-1930), born in Co. Antrim, was a plant collector of international renown. While working in the Chinese customs service from 1881 to 1900 he made excursions into unexplored parts of China and collected seeds and plant specimens unknown to European botanists. Among the plants that perpetuate his name are *Acer henryi, Spiraea henryi, Lilium henryi* and *Cotoneaster henryanus*.

ANSWER 92

(b) Honoré de Balzac, in a letter of 6 February 1844 to his lover, the Polish countess Éveline Hanska. Baron Georges Cuvier (1769-1832), the French zoologist and geologist, is regarded as the father of comparative anatomy and palaeontology (it was he, incidentally, who identified and named the pterodactyl).

The inclusion of Daniel O'Connell (1775-1847) in Balzac's list attests to the towering European reputation of one of the greatest Irishmen. Born in Derrynane, Co. Kerry, a place of singular beauty and serenity, O'Connell was educated in France. It is said that the atrocities he witnessed during the Revolution confirmed him as a pacifist. When he returned to Ireland, his exploits as a defence lawyer became legendary. His successful campaign for Catholic Emancipation was one of the epic battles for civil liberties in modern times and won him the accolade "The Liberator".

His marshalling of the masses of the Irish people to win, through agitation, political concessions from the Westminster parliament gives him a claim as strong as that of the American statesman, Andrew Jackson, to be the founder of modern mass democracy. A statue of O'Connell, who was a candidate for election as the first king of Belgium on its separation from the Netherlands in 1831, bestrides one of Europe's broadest boulevards—O'Connell Street, Dublin.

ANSWER 93

(c) twentieth. Over forty Japanese gardeners, under a Japanese head gardener, were engaged on their construction between 1906 and 1910. The original owner, Lord Wavertree, donated the entire property to the British Crown in 1915. After the foundation of the Irish state in 1922 the establishment continued, through an administrative quirk, as the British National Stud Company until 1943, when it was handed over to the Irish government, and became the Irish National Stud.

ANSWER 94

(c) 1986

Daniel O'Connell (1775-1847), one of the two greatest constitutional nationalist leaders.

Charles Stewart Parnell (1846-91), the other.

Éamon de Valera (1882-1975), above, born in New York, and Michael Collins (1890-1922), right, the two greatest revolutionary nationalist leaders of twentieth-century Ireland. Their disagreement over the Anglo-Irish Treaty of 1921 split nationalists and led to the formation of Fianna Fáil and Fine Gael.

Countess Markiewicz (1868-1927) was one of the commanders of the Citizen Army, founded by James Connolly, which took part in the Easter Rising, 1916. She was appointed Minister for Labour in the first Dáil.

James Larkin (1876-1947) who, along with James Connolly (1868-1916), led the Labour movement into the twentieth century. That movement submerged its political ambitions in the period 1916-1921 in the interest of national unity. When the new state emerged, Labour as a political force was therefore weak.

Edward Carson (1854-1935), left. A leader, with James Craig, of the Ulster Unionists, who, on his advice, accepted the Government of Ireland Act 1920, which set up a parliament for Northern Ireland.

James Craig (1871-1940), right, organised the Ulster Volunteers to resist Home Rule, by force if necessary. In 1921 he became the first Prime Minister of Northern Ireland.

Mrs Mary Robinson, at her inauguration as President of Ireland in Dublin Castle in 1990. The castle, splendidly refurbished by the Office of Public Works, is open to visitors.

John Hume, the leader of the majority nationalist party in Northern Ireland, the SDLP.

The British Prime Minister, John Major, and the Taoiseach, Albert Reynolds, making their Downing Street Declaration.

James Molyneaux, the leader of the majority Unionist party, the UUP.

A meeting of the European Council in Dublin in 1990. Membership of an increasingly integrating Europe is having profound effects on Irish political and social life.

QUESTION 95

Who said, *"There is no nation or people under the sun that doth love equal or indifferent* (i.e. impartial) *justice better than the Irish"*?

    Was it   (a) Richard Stanihurst (1545-1618), the first Irish writer of note to write in English?

                (b) Don Juan d'Aquilla, leader of the Spanish force at Kinsale in 1601?

                (c) Sir John Davies (1569-1626), the English Attorney General of Ireland under James I?

QUESTION 96

Who wrote:

> *This lovely land that always sent*
> *Her writers and artists to banishment*
> *And in the spirit of Irish fun*
> *Betrayed her own leaders, one by one?*

    Was it   (a) Patrick Kavanagh?
                (b) Louis MacNeice?
                (c) James Joyce?

QUESTION 97

What famous American economist said, *"All races have produced notable economists, with the exception of the Irish, who doubtless can protest their devotion to the higher arts"*?

    Was it   (a) J. Kenneth Galbraith?
                (b) Milton Friedman?
                (c) Paul Samuelson?

QUESTION 98

Irish troops have formed part of many United Nations peace-keeping missions (such as those to the Middle East, Cyprus, India, Pakistan and Lebanon). When did Ireland join the UN?

    Was it in   (a) 1955?
                  (b) 1960?
                  (c) 1965?

ANSWER 95

(c) Sir John Davies. Davies made his observation following the collapse of Gaelic Ireland in 1607. A marked feature of that society was the corpus of Brehon laws, with its finely gradated system of penalties. The pervasive influence of this legal code is corroborated by the fact that the practice of private Confession, with *its* finely gradated system of penances, was an invention of the early Christian community in Ireland. The principles of the Brehon law stretched back to a common Indo-European heritage. Thus in the absence of a state law enforcement system some moral mechanisms were needed to ensure a guilty person actually paid compensation. Fasting by the injured party at the door of the guilty party was sometimes used in both Ireland and India for this purpose. Curiously, in this century the hunger-strike has been used as a political weapon in both Ireland and India, notably by Terence Mac Swiney (1879-1920), nationalist lord mayor of Cork, and Mahatma Gandhi (1869-1948), the Indian nationalist leader and social reformer.

ANSWER 96

(c) James Joyce in "Gas from a Burner"

ANSWER 97

(a) J. Kenneth Galbraith (1908-), adviser to President Kennedy and US Ambassador to India (1961-63), in *The Age of Uncertainty*. Ireland is among the richest countries in the world. It is, however, among the four poorer countries of the European Union—Spain, Ireland, Greece and Portugal. It also has the highest economic growth rate in the Union, a position it has held for a number of years. Between 1971 and 1992, the real value of the goods and services it produced more than doubled; the increase was 118 per cent. That is almost double the growth, for the same period, of the EU as a whole (at 65 per cent) and of the USA (at 66 per cent). A great deal of the investment that has made this growth possible has come from outside Ireland (principally from the USA, Britain and Germany) and so there is a considerable outflow of profits from Ireland. In addition, the repayment of interest on foreign borrowings that financed the large increase in public spending in the late 1970s and early 1980s creates another substantial outflow. Nevertheless, the net increase in available resources during the period has been 96 per cent. Portugal is the only other EU country that has matched this performance. In the past few years, largely as a result of tight control of public expenditure, external debt as a proportion of Gross National Product (GNP) has been significantly reduced. This is consistent with the Maastricht guidelines. The rate of inflation is now less than 2%, and stable.

ANSWER 98

(a) 1955

QUESTION 99

John Scottus Eriugena, the Irish Neo-Platonist scholar featured on the Irish five-pound note, headed the school at the court of which French king?

Was it   (a) Charlemagne (742-814)?

           (b) Charles the Bald (823-877)?

           (c) Charles the Fat (839-888)?

QUESTION 100

This is the title of an Oscar-winning film by the Irish-American director John Ford, starring John Wayne and Maureen O'Hara. What is the missing word?

The Quiet _____

QUESTION 101

The earliest copyright case of which we have a record was heard in Ireland and concerned which one of the following books:

        (a) The *Cathach* or *Battle-book of the O'Donnells,* the earliest Irish manuscript extant and held in the Royal Irish Academy in Dublin?

        (b) The *Book of Kells, c.*900 AD, a copy of the Gospels on vellum and the most famous illuminated manuscript in the world, now on display in Trinity College, Dublin?

        (c) The *Annals of the Four Masters,* compiled between 1616 and 1636, a chronological history of Ireland in Irish from earliest times, and of which one of the two original copies, signed by its authors, is also held in the Royal Irish Academy?

QUESTION 102

Carrantuohill in Co. Kerry is the highest mountain in Ireland.

Is it over   (a) 1,000 metres?

           (b) 2,000 metres?

           (c) 3,000 metres?

ANSWER 99

(b) Charles the Bald. The philosopher, the greatest among those of his age, was famous for his wit. Once when he was in the group dining with the king, he being at one end of the table and the king at the other, the king could not resist making a pun at John Scottus Eriugena's expense: "Can anyone tell me the difference between an Irishman (*Scottus* in Latin) and a drunkard (*sottus*)?" John Scottus shot back: "The length of the table". Eriugena (the word means "born in Ireland") is to be distinguished from Duns Scotus (*c.*1270-1308), the famous Franciscan philosopher who was born in Scotland, and from whose name the word "dunce" is derived.

ANSWER 100

Man. Based on a short story by the Irish novelist Maurice Walsh (1879-1964) and set against the ravishing beauty of the west of Ireland, *The Quiet Man* is a rollicking piece of rustic burlesque quite different from Ford's normal genre, the western (*Stagecoach,* 1939; *She Wore a Yellow Ribbon,* 1949).

ANSWER 101

(a) The *Cathach,* a copy of the Psalms in Latin, traditionally ascribed to St Colmcille, who secretly transcribed it, prior to 600 AD, from a copy owned by St Finnian of Moville, Co. Donegal; St Finnian claimed that the copy made by Colmcille without permission belonged to him. The two saints repaired to Tara in Co. Meath where the High Kings of Ireland had their seat. The High King Dermot found in favour of St Finnian: "To every cow its calf and to every book its copy".

The king derived the principle from the Brehon laws, the corpus of Celtic law by which Ireland was governed for two millennia, from pre-Christian times to the destruction of the Gaelic system in 1607 AD. There was no law of copyright in the ancient classical world. Copyright, as we know it, emerged after the invention of printing in the fifteenth century. It was a by-product of the measures taken by public authorities to control this unprecedented means of spreading ideas: they insisted that printers register what they printed.

ANSWER 102

(a) At 1,040 metres, Carrantuohill is a modest mountain in global terms. Ben Nevis in Scotland, the highest mountain in Britain, rises to 1,342 metres. Mont Blanc, the highest peak in the Alps, rises to 4,808 metres. Most islands have highlands in the centre that slope to the sea. Ireland has a rich central plain that is contained by a rim of mountains. The central plain has considerable areas of bog as well as numerous rivers and lakes.

QUESTION 103

What Irish writer observed, "...*Kilbarrack, the healthiest graveyard in Ireland, they said, because it was so near the sea*"?

Was it   (a) Brendan Behan (1923-64), the author of *Borstal Boy* and *The Quare Fellow*?

(b) Frank O'Connor (1903-66), the short story writer acclaimed by Yeats as "the Irish Chekhov"?

(c) Patrick Kavanagh (1904-67), author of *Tarry Flynn* and *The Great Hunger*?

QUESTION 104

Round towers, all over a thousand years old, are to be found on the sites of how many early Christian monasteries in Ireland?

Is it   (a) nineteen?

(b) sixty-three?

(c) eighty-one?

QUESTION 105

In Ireland "The Year of the French" means the year in which General Jean-Joseph Humbert landed in Co. Mayo with a French army to assist the United Irishmen in their doomed rebellion against the English garrison in Ireland, led by Lord Cornwallis, who was to retrieve to some extent the reputation he had lost as British commander-in-chief in America.
Which of the following was "The Year of the French":

(a) 1796?

(b) 1797?

(c) 1798?

QUESTION 106

St Dympna, the patron saint of the insane, was the daughter of a seventh-century pagan Irish king. When little more than a child, she secretly became a Christian. When she reached the age of puberty, her crazed father made incestuous demands on her. She fled in horror with her confessor to a town in Belgium. Her father pursued her there and beheaded her himself when none of his aides would. The town developed a strong devotion to the saint—even today it has a church dedicated to her, Sint Dimpnakerk, on the site of her martyrdom. The town is renowned for its enlightened treatment of psychiatric patients. What is its name?

Is it   (a) Malines?

(b) Geel?

(c) Leuven?

ANSWER 103

(a) Brendan Behan. Kilbarrack is on the sea road from Dublin to Howth. The suburb of Kilbarrack is the inspiration for Barrytown, the locale of the trilogy of novels (*The Commitments, The Snapper, The Van*) by Roddy Doyle, the Dublin writer who won the Booker Prize in 1993 for his novel *Paddy Clarke Ha Ha Ha*. He is the first Irish writer to win the prize.

ANSWER 104

(b) sixty-three. About fifty kilometres south of Dublin is the stunningly beautiful site of the early Christian monastery of St Kevin in Glendalough ("the valley of the two lakes" in Irish). There you will find a round tower, a kind of building so singularly Irish that it figures among the national symbols. A round tower, soaring above the surrounding countryside, proclaimed the heavenly aspiration and permanence of a monastery. From its top, a bell, usually a hand-bell, would summon the monks from their individual cells or from the fields to communal prayer. The monks also used the round towers for the safe-keeping of manuscripts and reliquaries made of precious metals. In times of danger they rushed to the tower, scrambled up a rope ladder and slammed the door shut. Before the invention of gunpowder, a sealed round tower was virtually impregnable.

Some scholars believe the towers were built in the ninth century to provide the monks with a refuge from the marauding Vikings, who made their first assaults on Ireland at the close of the eighth century. However, the towers are strong and elegant buildings, hardly the product of haste and improvisation. Others believe they were built in the seventh century, that extraordinary period when Christian monasteries were founded all over Ireland. Before St Patrick's arrival, round buildings were traditional in Ireland. Because the Irish did not use mortar, the height to which they could raise stone buildings was very limited. Scholars who accept the earlier date of construction see the round towers as the glorious product of the Irish love of round structures and the discovery by the Irish of the use of mortar in late Roman Britain.

ANSWER 105

(c) 1798. The Irish-American writer Thomas Flanagan published a novel based on these events, *The Year of the French*, in 1979. It was made into a television mini-series in 1981 by Radio Telefís Éireann and France's FR3.

ANSWER 106

(b) Geel

QUESTION 107

In which of Shakespeare's plays does the following occur:
"...'tis like the howling of Irish wolves against the moon"?
>   Is it   (a) Two Gentlemen of Verona?
>   (b) Timon of Athens?
>   (c) As You Like It?

QUESTION 108

The actor William Grattan Tyrone Power was born in Waterford at the end of the eighteenth century (Power is one of the great Waterford names). During the 1830s, he played with brilliant success in American theatres. His great-grandson, the film star Tyrone Power (1914-58), represented the fourth generation of the family in the theatre. Another great-grandson was Tyrone Guthrie (1900-71), the renowned stage director, who bequeathed his home in Annaghmakerrig, Newbliss, Co. Monaghan as a centre where artists can go for short stretches to rest and work. The name "Tyrone" is Irish.
Was it originally the name of
>   (a) a place?
>   (b) an animal?
>   (c) a climatic feature?

QUESTION 109

The first cable link between Europe and America was established in 1866. Where in Ireland was the European terminal of the cable?
>   Was it in   (a) Donegal?
>   (b) Mayo?
>   (c) Kerry?

QUESTION 110

Which Irish writer said, "Satire is a sort of glass, wherein beholders do generally discover everybody's face but their own"?
>   Was it   (a) Oliver Goldsmith?
>   (b) Jonathan Swift?
>   (c) James Ussher?

QUESTION 111

Fáilte is the Irish word for "welcome": céad míle fáilte ("a hundred thousand welcomes") is a traditional greeting to visitors. The Irish Tourist Board is called felicitously Bord Fáilte. How many overseas visitors does the Republic receive annually?
>   Is it   (a) over two million?
>   (b) over three million?
>   (c) over four million?

ANSWER 107

(c) *As You Like It.* There are no large animals left in the wild in Ireland apart from deer. The last wolf was killed in Carlow in 1786 according to an account given by Robert Lloyd Praeger (1865-1953), a distinguished botanist born in Co. Down, the son of a Dutch linen merchant. The bear has been extinct for thousands of years, but visitors to the Aillwee Cave in Co. Clare can see pits where bears hibernated. The most spectacular animal bones recovered in Ireland are those of the Giant Irish Elk. You can see complete skeletons of these in the Natural History Museum in Dublin. Extinct for about ten thousand years, the Giant Irish Elk stood three metres high. The antlers of the male had a span of almost three metres.

ANSWER 108

(a) a place. It is an anglicisation of *Tír Eoghain* (Owen's country). Tyrone is one of the nine counties in Ulster.

ANSWER 109

(c) Kerry, on Valentia Island. The first transatlantic wireless signal was transmitted from Cornwall in England in 1901 by the Italian physicist Guglielmo Marconi (1874-1937), whose mother was Irish.

ANSWER 110

(b) Jonathan Swift in *The Battle of the Books.* Swift gave English the word "lilliputian" for someone or something diminutive (from Lilliput in *Gulliver's Travels*), the word "yahoo" for a boorish lout (from the class of animals in *Gulliver's Travels* with the forms of men but the understanding and passions of brutes), and the expression "a son of a gun" for a rake or hell-cat (from *The Battle of the Books*).

James Ussher (1581-1656), Protestant Archbishop of Armagh, became famous for a computation, based on his chronology of events in the Bible, that the world was created in 4004 BC.

ANSWER 111

(b) over three million (1992). It also receives over half-a-million visitors from Northern Ireland. As far as Britain's tourist markets are concerned, Ireland ranks fourth in terms of numbers (1992/93); moreover only visitors from the Middle East are economically more valuable to Britain than those from Ireland, who spend more per capita than Americans, Germans or French.

QUESTION 112

The National Museum in Kildare Street, Dublin, holds one of the largest and most important collections of Bronze Age gold in western Europe—the Ór ("gold" in Irish) collection. In addition, the museum houses magnificent pieces wrought in gold, silver and bronze from the early Christian era, such as the Tara Brooch, the Ardagh and Derrynaflan chalices, the Cross of Cong, the Crozier of Clonmacnois and St Patrick's Bell and Shrine. The immense quantity of Bronze Age gold objects emanating from Ireland suggests that rich ore sources once existed. Traces of gold still appear from time to time, and have occasionally caused considerable excitement among would-be prospectors. When did the last gold-rush occur in Ireland?

Was it in   (a) 1750?
              (b) 1805?
              (c) 1935?

QUESTION 113

Which Irish author wrote the song from which these lines come:

> *Dear Danny: I'm takin' this pen in me hand*
> *To tell you we're just out of sight of the land;*
> *In the grand Allen liner we're sailin' in style,*
> *But we're sailin' away from the Emerald Isle?*

Was it   (a) William Percy French (1854-1920), author of "The Mountains of Mourne"?
         (b) Alfred Percival Graves (1846-1931), author of "Father O'Flynn" and father of Robert Graves (*I Claudius, Claudius the God*)?
         (c) Lady Dufferin (1807-1867), grand-daughter of Richard Brinsley Sheridan, author of "The Emigrant's Lament"?

QUESTION 114

During the 1980s the British and Irish governments solemnly committed themselves in an Anglo-Irish Agreement, signed by the British Prime Minister, Mrs (now Baroness) Thatcher, and the Taoiseach, Dr Garret FitzGerald, to finding a peaceful solution to the problem of Northern Ireland which would respect both Unionist and Nationalist traditions.
In what year was the Agreement signed?

Was it   (a) 1980?
         (b) 1982?
         (c) 1985?

ANSWER 112

(c) 1935, in Co. Wicklow. This was a short-lived affair and not comparable to the gold-rush of the early nineteenth century, which was triggered by the finding of relatively significant amounts of gold in the vicinity of Croghan Kinsella Mountain in Co. Wicklow, and in the appropriately named Gold Mines River which flows down from it. (Incidentally, the biggest lead and zinc mine in western Europe is the Tara Mines outside Navan, Co. Meath. It is owned by a Finnish mining company.)

ANSWER 113

(a) William Percy French, in "The Emigrant's Letter". For almost two hundred years emigration has been a marked feature of Irish society. Since Independence, emigration has fluctuated annually between five and fifteen per thousand of the population except for a short period in the 1960s when it was halted and reversed.

ANSWER 114

(c) 1985. On 15 December 1993, the Taoiseach, Albert Reynolds and the British Prime Minister, John Major, in their Downing Street Declaration set forth a balanced framework for peace in Northern Ireland.

QUESTION 115

Which person of Irish descent said, "*The only good Indian is a dead Indian*"?
Was it   (a) Wild Bill Hickok?
           (b) Andrew Jackson?
           (c) General Phil Sheridan?

QUESTION 116

Which statesman, born in Ireland, said, "*...the age of chivalry is gone. That of sophisters, economists, and calculators has succeeded; and the glory of Europe is extinguished forever*"?
Was it   (a) Daniel O'Connell (1775-1847), born in Kerry?
           (b) Arthur Wellesley, Duke of Wellington (1769-1852), born in Dublin?
           (c) Edmund Burke (1729-97), born in Dublin?

QUESTION 117

What are the colours of the Irish tricolour?
Are they   (a) green, white and orange?
            (b) green, white and gold?
            (c) green, white and red?

QUESTION 118

Colonel James Fitzmaurice, a Dublinman, resigned from the Royal Air Force in Britain, in which he had served with distinction, to join the Irish Army Air Corps formed after the foundation of the state in 1922. Some years later, Fitzmaurice and two German aviators, Baron von Huenefeld and Captain Koehl, took off from Baldonnel aerodrome near Dublin to make the first flight from east to west across the Atlantic against the prevailing winds. They landed on a frozen lake in Labrador over thirty-six hours later. When did they make the flight?
Was it in   (a) 1924?
            (b) 1926?
            (c) 1928?

ANSWER 115

(c) General Phil Sheridan (1831-88). Sheridan, whose parents came from Cavan, was commander of the Union cavalry in the American civil war. He destroyed the Confederate supply lines in Shenandoah in 1864 and, by cutting off General Robert E. Lee's retreat, forced the South's surrender. After the war he was made commander of the Army of the West which oversaw the destruction of the Plains Indians. The statement gave rise to the equally heartless twentieth-century formulation "The only good commie is a dead commie!" It is probable that Sheridan actually said "The only good Indians I ever saw were dead".

ANSWER 116

(c) Edmund Burke in *Reflections on the Revolution in France*. One of the outstanding orators of modern times, Burke declared in his speech in the British House of Commons on conciliation with America, "All government, indeed every human benefit and enjoyment, every virtue, and every prudent act, is founded on compromise and barter".

ANSWER 117

(a) green, white and orange. In 1848, a deputation of the nationalist Young Ireland movement returned from France bringing with them a tricolour, inspired by the French *tricoleur*: the green represented the majority, old native, mainly Catholic population; the orange represented the minority, mainly Northern-located, Protestant population whose ascendancy in Ireland had been established by King William (of Orange) after his victory over King James II at the Battle of the Boyne, 1690 (the last occasion two kings confronted one another on a European battlefield); and the white represented the desired harmony between the two groups. Later nationalist movements showed little interest in the tricolour. However, it was adopted by Sinn Féin ("Ourselves Alone"—an expression of self-reliance), the organisation that became the vehicle through which Ireland achieved independence. In the Easter Rising, 1916, more than half the flags flown over the strongpoints in Dublin occupied by the insurgents were tricolours (the others being the green flag bearing either a harp or the text "Irish Republic"). In the transformation of public attitudes that followed the execution of the leaders of the Rising by the British, support consolidated behind Sinn Féin, and the tricolour became identified as the national flag. Following the ratification of the Anglo-Irish Treaty in 1922, the new Irish government formally recognised the tricolour as the national flag.

ANSWER 118

(c) 1928

QUESTION 119

The ancient Irish, being a pastoral people, set great store by periodic gatherings or fairs where they could conduct business and enjoy rumbustious socialising. Some of these fairs are still held. Puck Fair, which is presided over by a wild he-goat ensconced on a high platform (an hilariously incongruous vestige of ancient pagan fertility rites), is held in Killorglin, Co. Kerry, from 10 to 12 August. At the Oul' Lammas Fair in Ballycastle, Co. Antrim, held in late August, you are exhorted in the words of the old song "to treat your Mary Anne to dulse and yellow man". Dulse is an edible seaweed. What is yellow man?

Is it   (a) chocolate?
          (b) sweet cake?
          (c) toffee?

QUESTION 120

Lough Neagh is the largest lake in Ireland. How large is it in comparison with other European lakes?

Is it the   (a) fourth largest?
            (b) tenth largest?
            (c) eighteenth largest?

QUESTION 121

The Irish constitution obliges the state to ensure the provision of free education for all at primary level. Distinct sections of society are entitled to manage schools that reflect their own ethos and values. Thus, while most primary schools are under Catholic management, there are Protestant schools, and interdenominational, Jewish, and Moslem schools. There is also a network of schools throughout the country which provides education at first and second levels entirely through the medium of the Irish language.

The importance attached to education in Irish culture is evident in the peace negotiations (1644-48) which took place between the Confederation of Kilkenny—a national assembly established in Ireland during the civil war in England—and Dublin Castle, the centre of English power. Educational clauses, by which the Irish sought to ensure freedom in educational matters, were a serious bone of contention. (Previously Hugh O'Neill, the Irish leader, had unsuccessfully looked for similar guarantees from Queen Elizabeth in negotiations during the Nine Years War, 1594-1603.) Education had not yet arisen as an issue elsewhere in Europe. In fact, educational clauses do not enter into European peace treaties until the twentieth century. In the Republic, education at both first and second levels is free. While education at third level is not, it is heavily supported by the state. What proportion of each year's age group enrols for third-level education in Ireland?

Is it   (a) 23%?
          (b) 36%?
          (c) 42%?

ANSWER 119

(c) toffee. The word Lammas comes from Old English *hláfmaesse* and means "loaf mass". Donnybrook is a suburb of Dublin. The fair held annually there since 1204 became so noted for its disorder that "Donnybrook" has entered English as a term for a scene of general uproar. Donnybrook Fair was suppressed in 1855.

ANSWER 120

(c) the eighteenth largest. Russia contains some of the largest lakes in Europe, including the largest, Lake Ladoga (18,518 sq km). After Russia, Europe's most extensive lakes are to be found in the Scandinavian countries of Sweden (Lakes Väner, Vätter, Mälar) and Finland (Lakes Inari, Paijanne, Oulu järvi and Saimaa). Excluding both the Russian and Scandinavian lakes, Lake Balaton (689 sq km) in Hungary is Europe's largest lake, followed by Lake Constance (531 sq km) between Switzerland and Germany, and Lake Geneva (578 sq km) between Switzerland and France. Next is Lough Neagh (392 sq km). Lough Neagh, which borders five of the six counties of Northern Ireland, was formed, according to legend, in the first century AD when a magical well, which had been carelessly left uncovered, overflowed and flooded the surrounding countryside. Thomas Moore recalls the legend in "Let Erin Remember the Days of Old":

> *On Lough Neagh's banks, as the fisherman strays*
> *When the clear cold eve 's declining*
> *He sees the round towers of other days*
> *In the water beneath him shining.*

Lough Neagh (from the Irish *Loch nEachach*) literally means "the lake abounding in horses".

ANSWER 121

(b) 36%. The corresponding percentages in some other European countries are: France 50%, Germany 45%, Sweden 40%, Spain 33%, United Kingdom 20%, Poland 12%, Hungary 10%.

Hugh Lane (1875-1915), above left, born in Co. Cork. A distinguished art connoisseur, he put together a collection of thirty-nine modern European works that included such masterpieces of Impressionism as *Les Parapluies,* above, by Renoir. He intended to leave the collection to Dublin, if the city fathers provided a suitable place to hang them. Lane was returning from a business trip to America on board the *Lusitania* when it was sunk off the Cork coast by a German submarine. He was last seen helping women and children into the boats. (The sinking of the *Lusitania,* with the loss of more than a hundred American passengers, helped bring the USA into World War I.) A dispute over Lane's will ended in an agreement in 1959 whereby about half the collection is held in the Municipal Art Gallery in Dublin and the rest is held in the National Gallery in London, and an exchange is made roughly every seven years.

Lady Gregory (1852-1932), centre left, was Hugh Lane's aunt. A founding director of the Abbey Theatre with WB Yeats, she was an influential figure in the great literary renaissance at the beginning of the twentieth century. The plays produced at the Abbey were a glorious expression of that movement. Among the playwrights of genius whose works were produced by the Abbey was Seán O'Casey, seen, left, with the actress Ria Mooney in 1926 when his play *The Plough and the Stars* was first presented.

'The Taking of Christ' by Michelangelo Amerighi da Caravaggio (1573-1610), one of the treasures of the National Gallery of Ireland. The National Gallery holds the greatest single collection of Irish art. In addition it has a collection of the great masters—Vermeer, Velázquez, Rubens, Titian, David, Uccello, Rembrandt, Poussin—which in range and quality makes it comparable to the other leading galleries in Europe.

Untitled work by Mainie Jellett (1876-1944) from the Irish Museum of Modern Art. The museum is housed in the Royal Hospital, Kilmainham, Dublin, the finest seventeenth-century building in Ireland. Modelled on Les Invalides in Paris, it was restored by the Office of Public Works in 1984.

QUESTION 122

In what novel does the following passage occur:
"...*Ireland, they say, has the honour of being the only country which never persecuted the Jews. Do you know why?*
—*Why, sir? Stephen asked.*
—*Because she never let them in, Mr Deasy replied solemnly.*"

Is it   (a) *The Untilled Field* by George Moore?
      (b) *At Swim-Two-Birds* by Flann O'Brien?
      (c) *Ulysses* by James Joyce?

QUESTION 123

"Doing pana" is a common expression in Cork city.
Does it mean   (a) serving a sentence with hard labour in Limerick jail?
      (b) baking Irish soda bread?
      (c) promenading along St Patrick's Street in Cork?

QUESTION 124

Yeats, in *The Winding Stair and Other Poems*, sang of the sisters Eva and Constance Gore-Booth:

> *Two girls in silk kimonos, both*
> *Beautiful, one a gazelle.*

Constance married a Polish count and it was as Countess Markiewicz that she became the first woman to be elected a Member of Parliament (MP) in the British House of Commons. She did not take her seat at Westminster but instead in the first Dáil in Dublin, and became a minister in the first government appointed by Dáil Éireann in 1919. When was she elected to Westminster?
Was it in   (a) 1906?
      (b) 1913?
      (c) 1918?

QUESTION 125

In 1991, the number of births per thousand of the population was 10.4 in Germany, 13.3 in France, 13.7 in the UK, 9.6 in Italy. What was the figure in Ireland?
Was it   (a) 11.0?
      (b) 13.0?
      (c) 15.0?

Answer 122

(c) *Ulysses* by James Joyce. Ireland's Jewish population is tiny—fewer than two thousand of the Republic's citizens are Jews. But the Jewish contribution to Irish life is disproportionately large. Thus currently three of the Dáil's 166 deputies are Jewish and one of them is a member of the government. Incidentally, Chaim Herzog, President of Israel (1983-93), is Irish—he was born in Belfast.

James Joyce had many Jewish friends. When the writer fled Paris in 1940, one of these, Paul Léon, returned to Joyce's flat, sorted out his papers and placed them for safe keeping with the Irish legation in the city. Tragically, Léon was caught in a Nazi round-up of Jews shortly afterwards and sent to a concentration camp, where he died in 1942. He had delayed his departure from Paris until his son had sat his baccalauréat examination.

Answer 123

(c) promenading along St Patrick's Street. This is a traditional exercise for the young people of both sexes, which allows them to size each other up and get to know each other. The Irish word *corcach*, whence the name "Cork", means a low-lying swampy place, and it was on a small island here that St Finbarr (from whom we get the first name "Barry") founded his monastery in the seventh century. Even today, the two finest streets, St Patrick's Street and Grand Parade, are built over broad and deep pools where merchant ships berthed in the eighteenth century.

There are many words and expressions in Irish speech which are distinctive. "On the batter", meaning "on the spree" (*spraoi* in Irish means "fun", "frolic') originated in Dublin, where the eighteenth-century rakes were wont to resort to the inns in the district of Stoney*batter*. Other Irish language words surviving in colloquial speech are *plámás* (flattery), *flahoolagh* (hospitable), and *meas* (regard, esteem). Visitors to Ireland may see notices advertising a *fleá ceoil* (pronounced "flah keoil'), which means a festival of Irish traditional music, where among other instruments, they will probably hear the *bodhrán* (pronounced "bowrawn'), a cross between a drum and a tambourine.

Answer 124

(c) 1918

Answer 125

(c) 15.0, the highest in the EU

QUESTION 126

Bunratty Castle, the former seat of the O'Briens of Thomond, near Shannon Airport, now hosts a famous medieval entertainment for visitors. Who said of Bunratty at the height of its noble splendour, "*I have no hesitation in asserting that Bunratty is the most beautiful spot I have ever seen. In Italy there is nothing like the palace and grounds of Lord Thomond, nothing like its ponds and park, with its three thousand head of deer*"?

Was it   (a) Archbishop Rinuccini, Papal Nuncio to the Confederation of Kilkenny (1645-49)?

                (b) the Englishman Edmund Campion in *A History of Ireland* (1571)?

                (c) Alexis de Tocqueville, the French sociologist and traveller, in his *Journeys to England and Ireland*, who visited Ireland in 1833 and 1835?

QUESTION 127

In 1990, the number of deaths per thousand of the population was 11.9 in Denmark, 11.5 in Germany, 11.2 in the UK, 10.0 in Luxembourg, 8.6 in both the Netherlands and Spain. What was it in Ireland?

Was it   (a) 8.1?

                (b) 9.1?

                (c) 10.1?

QUESTION 128

The Three Sisters are three important geographical features in Ireland.

Are they   (a) rivers?

                (b) mountains?

                (c) lakes?

QUESTION 129

What Irish playwright said, "*A man may surely be allowed to take a glass of wine by his own fireside*"?

Was it   (a) Richard Brinsley Sheridan?

                (b) Hugh Leonard?

                (c) Charles Macklin?

ANSWER 126

(a) Archbishop Rinuccini

ANSWER 127

(b) 9.1, the third lowest in the EU after the Netherlands and Spain

ANSWER 128

(a) rivers. The Barrow, Nore and Suir rise within twenty miles of each other, the Barrow and Nore in Co. Offaly in the Slieve Bloom Mountains, and the Suir in Co. Tipperary at the Devil's Bit Mountain. All three rise in beautiful surroundings. A famous fishing river, the Suir flows through the Golden Vale, in the middle of which the Rock of Cashel rises like an acropolis. Legend has it that the Rock of Cashel was formed when the Devil, having taken a bite out of the Devil's Bit Mountain as he flew past, dropped it on the plain. From Cashel (a "rock fort" in Irish), the early Gaels ruled the province of Munster. Today, the architectural remains on the Rock include a round tower, a roofless cathedral, the stone Cross of St Patrick, and Cormac's Chapel. Cormac's Chapel, which dates from 1134, is called after Cormac Mac Carthy, who was both a bishop and king of Munster. The Chapel is one of the finest examples of Hiberno-Romanesque art.

The Barrow and Nore rise in adjoining valleys in the Slieve Bloom Mountains, an inland region of outstanding natural beauty, with many glens, forested slopes and mountain heath. In this beautiful and secluded area the legendary Fionn Mac Cool was brought up in secret, safe from the venom of his enemies, the Clann Morna, who had slain his father. Much later, the area provided refuge for the Costigans, who took to the hills as rapparees (dispossessed owners turned outlaw) when deprived of their lands in the Cromwellian confiscations of the seventeenth century. Having gone their separate ways, the three rivers, the storied sisters, come together to greet the sea in Waterford harbour.

ANSWER 129

(a) Richard Brinsley Sheridan (1751-1816), author of *The Rivals* and *The School for Scandal*. He made the observation on being accosted while drinking a glass of wine in the street, as he watched the Drury Lane Theatre in London, which he had just restored, go up in flames.

QUESTION 130

Dublin, Ireland's capital city, is situated at 53.21° north latitude. One of the following cities is more northerly.

Is it   (a) Quebec?
        (b) Warsaw?
        (c) Hamburg?

QUESTION 131

The centuries-old struggle for Irish independence ended with the signing of an Anglo-Irish Treaty in London in 1921. One of the signatories on the Irish side declared: *"Think what I have got for Ireland! Something which she has wanted these past seven hundred years. Will anyone be satisfied with the bargain? Will anyone? I tell you this—early this morning I signed my own death warrant"*.

Was it   (a) Arthur Griffith?
        (b) Erskine Childers?
        (c) Michael Collins?

QUESTION 132

Irish surnames fall mainly into two broad categories—those beginning with "O' " (O'Donnell, O'Sullivan, O'Kelly, etc) and those beginning with "Mac" or "Mc" (MacCarthy, MacCormack, MacNamara, etc). "O" means "grandson of" or "descendant of" and "Mac" means "son of". Surnames came into general use in Ireland at a comparatively early date.

Was that   (a) the ninth century?
         (b) the eleventh century?
         (c) the fourteenth century?

QUESTION 133

The Celts, who once dominated central and western Europe, have left traces of their occupation throughout those regions. The name Vienna comes from the Celtic "Findubona", the first element of which is the same as the name of the mythical Irish hero Fionn. The word *fionn* in Irish means "fair" or "clear" (the Phoenix Park in Dublin takes its name not from the mythical bird but from *fionnuisce*, meaning "clear water", which was to be got from a well within its confines; the well is still there). The Irish *fionn* is closely related to "find" in English, a fact which stems from the Indo-European origins of both languages. Which other European capital city has a name of Celtic origin?

Is it   (a) Dublin?
       (b) London?
       (c) Paris?

ANSWER 130

(c) Hamburg (53.33°n). Ireland is situated to the north-west of the continent of Europe between 51.5° and 55.5°. Since it lies in the path of mild south-westerly winds and is washed by warm water drifting up from the Gulf of Mexico, it has an equable climate: never too warm or too cold, too dry or too wet. So, when James Joyce, in the elegiac finale to his greatest short story "The Dead", filmed memorably in 1987 by the Irish-American director John Huston, says, "Yes, the papers were right: snow was general all over Ireland", he was referring to a relatively infrequent phenomenon. Snow, when it does occur, is rarely prolonged or severe.

ANSWER 131

(c) Michael Collins (1890-1922), one of the legendary guerilla leaders of modern times. The Treaty, which provided for the partitioning of Ireland between a twenty-six county Irish Free State with its capital in Dublin and a six-county Northern Ireland with its capital in Belfast, split the Irish nationalists and led to a civil war, 1922-23. Collins, then the Irish Free State army chief, was killed in an ambush in his native county, Cork.

ANSWER 132

(b) the eleventh century, following an edict of Brian Boru (941-1014), king of Ireland, who crushed the Danes at the Battle of Clontarf, 1014. The ruling families, jealous of their genealogies, which legitimised their authority, often derived their new surnames from a distinguished ancestor in earlier centuries. Thus the O'Neill surname (which means "descendant of Niall") shows descent from Niall of the Nine Hostages, a High King who ruled at Tara in Co. Meath from 380 to 405 AD. Similarly, the descendants of Brian Boru demonstrated their illustrious descent by becoming O'Briens. ("Boru" derives from the Irish *bóramha* "a levy of cattle", traditionally imposed by the High King on the province of Leinster. Brian got the nickname when in 1002, having usurped the High Kingship, he re-imposed the levy.) "Mac" shows more immediate descent. It is also the general indicator of Gaelic names in Scotland.

ANSWER 133

All three. Dublin derives from the Irish *dubh* "black" and *linn* "pool'; the Black Pool, now covered in, was in Dame Street near City Hall. However, the name now used for Dublin in Irish—Baile Átha Cliath—derives from a more ancient period. It means "the town of the hurdle-ford" (the ford on the Liffey was located within a kilometre of the "Black Pool"). Another ancient name for Dublin is Eblana. It is found on Ptolemy's map and may be a corruption of a Latinised version of *Dubh Linn*. London, originally *Londinium*, was derived by the Romans from a Celtic placename, the origin of which is uncertain. Paris derives from the Latin *Lutetia Parisorum* "the marshes of the Parisi", a Celtic tribe. (Lutetia is the name used for Paris in the French cartoon strip *Asterix*.)

QUESTION 134

Anagram: E E T L V N N I A
A renowned friend of lovers

QUESTION 135

One of the following buildings was designed by an Irishman.
Was it   (a) the Winter Palace in St Petersburg?
          (b) the Elysée Palace in Paris?
          (c) the White House in Washington?

QUESTION 136

Unemployment and its concomitant poverty are the most serious economic and social problems facing Ireland. The major factors at play in Irish unemployment are as follows. Ireland proportionately has far more people employed in farming than any other EU country apart from Greece and Portugal; technology has had such an impact on farming that there are fewer and fewer jobs available in agriculture every year. The increase in Ireland's industrial output has come from high-tech, capital-intensive activities with high productivity and relatively few jobs. Ireland's birth-rate is higher than that of any other EU country so that relatively more young people come on the job market each year. Service industries, such as tourism, banking, insurance, education and entertainment, are only at a medium level of development. In recent years recession in Britain and the US, traditional providers of job opportunities for Irish people, means not only that people who might have emigrated do not, but that many who have emigrated return. Ireland (1993) has the second highest level of unemployment in the EU.
Is it   (a) 18%?
         (b) 19%?
         (c) 20%?

QUESTION 137

Cyrano de Bergerac (1619-55), the eponymous hero of the work by Edmond Rostand (1868-1918), was a French writer and soldier, famous as a duellist and for his prominent proboscis. Arras, a town in Northern France, from which English derives the word arras for a wall tapestry, was then in the Spanish Netherlands. The commander of the Spaniards who, historically, defended the town against the assault of Cyrano and the French was an Irishman.
Was he   (a) Owen Roe O'Neill?
          (b) Thomas Preston?
          (c) Patrick Sarsfield?

ANSWER 134

Valentine. On 14 February—St Valentine's Day—lovers exchange earnests of their mutual passion. Valentine was a Christian martyr beheaded in Rome towards the end of the third century. He became associated with the celebration of love because his feast coincided with the great pagan Spring festival in Rome—the Saturnalia, called after Saturn, the old Roman god of fertility. The bones of St Valentine now rest far from Rome in a small gilded casket in the Carmelite church in Whitefriar Street in Dublin. They were a gift from Pope Gregory XVI in 1836 in appreciation of the work of the saintly prior of Whitefriar Street, Father John Spratt.

ANSWER 135

(c) the White House in Washington. In 1790 a decision was made by the first US Congress to establish a federal capital on the Potomac river. In a public competition to choose a design for the President's residence, an Irish architect from Co. Kilkenny who had settled in Philadelphia, James Hoban, was the winner. It is said that Hoban derived elements of his design from Leinster House, the residence of the Dukes of Leinster in Kildare Street, Dublin, and now the seat of the two houses of the Irish parliament (the Dáil and Seanad). Work on the new capital—and the President's house—went slowly, and Washington never lived there. When the government finally moved to the new city in 1800, President Adams took up residence in the still unfinished building. The building was partly destroyed in the course of war with the British in 1814. Afterwards, it was found impossible to clean the walls blackened by smoke, so Hoban suggested that the entire exterior be painted white. The solution was accepted—and gave the house its name.

ANSWER 136

(b) 19%. Spain at 19.5% is highest. The EU average is 10.6%.

ANSWER 137

(a) Owen Roe O'Neill, a nephew of Hugh O'Neill, the great Ulster chief who, with his neighbouring Donegal ally Red Hugh O'Donnell, was defeated by the English at Kinsale, Co Cork, in 1601. The flight of the two Hughs with other Irish nobles to the continent in 1607, known as the Flight of the Earls, brought Gaelic Ireland crashing down.

QUESTION 138

The novel is the only literary form that was not invented by the ancient classical writers—hence the use of the word "novel" which ultimately derives from the Latin *novus* "new". *Don Quixote* by Miguel de Cervantes (1547-1616) and *Pamela* by Samuel Richardson (1689-1761) were the earliest significant works in the genre in Spain and England respectively. Maria Edgeworth (1767-1849) was the first significant Irish novelist writing in English. Which of the following was her first novel?

Was it   (a) *Castle Rackrent*?
               (b) *Forgive and Forget*?
               (c) *Rosanna?*

QUESTION 139

Gaeltacht, or Irish-speaking, areas are to be found in a number of counties. Is that number   (a) three?
                   (b) five?
                   (c) seven?

QUESTION 140

What Irishman, as he lay dying, replied to his doctor who had told him he was coughing "with more difficulty", "*That is surprising, since I have been practising all night!*" Was it   (a) John Philpot Curran?
                   (b) Napper Tandy?
                   (c) Daniel O'Connell?

QUESTION 141

Anagram: T L F I L M N O E
A great monastery

QUESTION 142

In 1880, at the height of the Irish tenant farmers' struggle against landlordism, a land agent called Captain Boycott refused to reduce rents following a bad harvest. His outraged tenants ostracised him: no labourer would work for him, no servant would cook for him, no one would pay him rent. Six policemen had to be assigned to guard him. After six months he packed up and left for England with his family. This episode, made into a film, *Captain Boycott* (1947), starring Stewart Grainger, gave English the verb "to boycott". In which west of Ireland county did the episode take place?

Was it   (a) Clare?
               (b) Mayo?
               (c) Sligo?

ANSWER 138

(a) *Castle Rackrent.* The first novel written in Irish was *Stair Éamainn Uí Chléire* by Seán Ó Neachtain (1655-1728); it was not published, however, until 1918.

ANSWER 139

(c) seven. They are Cork, Donegal, Galway, Kerry, Mayo, Meath and Waterford. There are perhaps 35,000 people (one per cent of the Republic's population) in those areas whose vernacular is Irish. All Irish school children learn to speak, read and write Irish. English, however, is the prevalent language.

ANSWER 140

(a) John Philpot Curran. It was Curran (1750-1817) who said, "The condition upon which God hath given liberty to man is eternal vigilance", in a speech on the election of the Lord Mayor of Dublin in 1790. Curran's daughter Sarah was secretly engaged to the Irish patriot, Robert Emmet, who was executed in 1803. Thomas Moore's song, "She is far from the land where her young hero sleeps", was inspired by her tragic story.

ANSWER 141

Mellifont. Founded in 1142, Mellifont, near Drogheda in Co. Louth, was the first Cistercian Abbey in Ireland and was modelled, even to its riverside location, on the famous Cistercian Abbey of Clairvaux in France which was founded by St Bernard only twenty-seven years before. Mellifont in time came to be known as the Great Monastery because as many as thirty houses, including Baltinglass, Boyle and Shrule, were offshoots of it. The Abbey was suppressed in 1539 at the time of the Reformation, and came into the possession of the ancestors of Henry Moore, Earl of Drogheda, after whom Henry Street, Moore Street and Earl Street in Dublin are named.

ANSWER 142

(b) Mayo

QUESTION 143

Ireland is largely dependent on external sources for its energy supplies. The Republic has no operating coal-mines or commercial oil-wells. It does have a natural gas field off Kinsale in Co. Cork, abundant supplies of turf (peat) and waterpower. The Electricity Supply Board (ESB), the state company that generates and distributes nearly all electricity, depends on a variety of energy sources: gas 25 per cent, oil 16 per cent, peat 14 per cent, hydro 5 per cent, coal 40 per cent. The ESB was established in 1927 and immediately undertook the development of the Shannon hydro-electric scheme, one of the largest engineering projects ever undertaken in the state. They were assisted by a major foreign company.
Was that company
(a) Westinghouse (USA)?
(b) Siemens (Germany)?
(c) Brown Boveri (Switzerland)?

QUESTION 144

One of these plays was first written in English.
Was it (a) *The Hostage* by Brendan Behan?
(b) *Waiting for Godot* by Samuel Beckett?
(c) *Dancing at Lughnasa* by Brian Friel?

QUESTION 145

In 1991, the number of marriages per thousand of the population was 6.1 in Belgium, 6.3 in the Netherlands, 7.3 in Portugal. What was it in Ireland?
Was it (a) 4.8?
(b) 5.8?
(c) 6.8?

QUESTION 146

Who said, "*In Ireland the inevitable never happens and the unexpected constantly occurs*"?
Was it (a) Oscar Wilde?
(b) John Pentland Mahaffy, Oscar Wilde's professor in Trinity College Dublin?
(c) Dr William Wilde, Oscar Wilde's father?

ANSWER 143

(b) Siemens

ANSWER 144

(c) *Dancing at Lughnasa. Waiting for Godot* was first written in French. *The Hostage* was first written in Irish.

ANSWER 145

(a) 4.8, the lowest in the EU

ANSWER 146

(b) John Pentland Mahaffy (1839-1919). Mahaffy, once asked to differentiate between Irish bulls and other bulls, observed, "Irish bulls are always pregnant". A notable example of Ireland's ability to produce the unexpected occurred after the Young Ireland rising of 1848, when many of those involved were transported to Van Diemen's Land as felons or had to flee the country with a price on their heads. Lord Chief Justice Blackburne was so incensed at the nonchalance shown by four of those brought to trial that he condemned them to the medieval horror of being hanged, drawn and quartered. Passionate appeals led Queen Victoria to commute their sentence to transportation to the penal colony of Australia. In 1873 the Queen was astounded to learn that Charles Gavan Duffy (1816-1903), prime minister of Victoria, Australia, whom she was about to honour with a knighthood, had been one of the Young Ireland leaders. Curious, she enquired what had become of the others.

It transpired that Kevin Izod O'Doherty (1824-1905) had become a member of the Legislative Assembly and Council of Queensland; that Thomas D'Arcy McGee (1825-68) had become president of the Council of the Dominion of Canada; that Thomas Meagher (1825-67), nicknamed "Meagher of the Sword" by Thackeray, had become governor of Montana in the United States; that Richard O'Gorman (1826-95) had become a judge of the Superior Court of New York; that John Mitchel (1815-75) had become a newspaper publisher and editor in America; that Michael Doheny (1805-62), a lawyer, had become lieutenant-colonel of the 69th Regiment, New York State Militia ("the Fighting 69th"); and that Patrick Smyth (1822-85) had been conferred with the Legion of Honour by the French government in 1871.

QUESTION 147

Aer Rianta is the state agency in the Republic responsible for the management of Dublin, Shannon and Cork airports. Its subsidiary, Aer Rianta International, has duty-free outlets or management contracts in a number of overseas locations, for example Warsaw, Bahrain and Karachi, as well as in which of these cities:

      (a) Moscow?
      (b) St Petersburg?
      (c) Kiev?

QUESTION 148

What British statesman said, *"There were indeed Irish Roman Catholics of great ability, energy, and ambition; but they were to be found everywhere except in Ireland: at Versailles and at Saint Ildefonso, in the armies of Frederick and of Maria Theresa...Scattered all over Europe were to be found brave Irish generals, dexterous Irish diplomatists, Irish Counts, Irish Barons, Irish Knights of St Louis and of St Leopold, of the White Eagle and of the Golden Fleece, who, if they had remained in the house of bondage* [their native land] *could not have been ensigns of marching regiments nor freemen of petty corporations"*?

Was it   (a) William Pitt the Younger (1759-1806)?
         (b) Lord Macaulay (1800-59)?
         (c) Joseph Chamberlain (1836-1914)?

QUESTION 149

In 1990, the density of population per sq km was 361.7 in the Netherlands, 327.4 in Belgium, 235.5 in the UK, 77.3 in Greece.
What was it in Ireland?

Was it   (a) 40.0?
         (b) 50.0?
         (c) 60.0?

QUESTION 150

What famous German writer observed, *"Eighteen months before Lenin took over the remains of an empire, the Irish poets were scraping away the first stone from under the pedestal of that other empire which was regarded as indestructible but has since turned out to be far from it "*?

Was it   (a) Günther Grass?
         (b) Berthold Brecht?
         (c) Heinrich Böll?

ANSWER 147

All three. Aer Rianta means Air Tracks in Irish. Aer Lingus means Air Fleet in Irish.

ANSWER 148

(b) Lord Macaulay, in his *History of England*. The penal laws were a series of enactments, introduced in the years following the triumph of William of Orange at the Battle of the Boyne in 1690, which penalised the majority of the Irish population because they were Catholic; to a lesser degree they also militated against Ulster Presbyterians. The penal laws did not directly prohibit the practice of the Catholic religion but subjected it to harsh conditions. The laws had a political and economic motive, which was to penalise the Catholic majority, by keeping them in penury, as long as they retained their links with France and Spain in religious matters. Catholics were prohibited from buying land or from leasing it for more than thirty-one years. So, by the end of the eighteenth century, barely five per cent of the land of Ireland remained in Catholic hands. The Catholic Irish emigrated in great numbers to Spain, Austria, Italy, Germany, Russia and, especially, France. Between 1691, when General Patrick Sarsfield departed for France with 12,000 of his 15,000 Irish troops, and the Battle of Fontenoy in 1745, tens of thousands of Irishmen died in the service of France alone.

ANSWER 149

(b) 50.0, the lowest in the EU

ANSWER 150

(c) Heinrich Böll (1917-85), in his *Irish Journal*. Born in Cologne, he won the Nobel Prize for Literature in 1972. In his will, he left his cottage in the wild beauty of Achill Island in Mayo for the use of visiting artists. The Easter Rising of 1916 (sometimes called "The Poets' Revolution"), centred on the General Post Office in Dublin, was led by an idealistic group, among whom were the poets PH Pearse and Thomas MacDonagh.

Public revulsion at the execution of the leaders of the insurrection (the wounded James Connolly was strapped into a chair before being shot) created a wave of nationalist passion that swept the British out of Ireland—or most of it—within six years.

The Chieftains is one of the groups of Irish musicians which came to the fore in the 1960s. They have toured as far afield as China, playing traditional Irish instruments—fiddle, flute, harp, bodhrán and uilleann pipes. Some of their most memorable work has been with Belfast-born Van Morrison on the *Irish Heartbeat* album.

Sinéad O'Connor, Ireland's enchanting but tempestuous chanteuse.

U2, formed in 1976 when its members were still schoolboys, is the most successful rock band to come from Ireland.

Liam Neeson from Ballymena, Co. Antrim, as Oskar Schindler, and Ben Kingsley in Steven Spielberg's film *Schindler's List,* based on the bestselling book, *Schindler's Ark*, by the Irish-Australian writer Thomas Keneally.

Alison Doody, the Dublin-born film actress who starred in the James Bond film *A View to a Kill* and in *Indiana Jones and the Last Crusade.*

The Limerick-born film star, Richard Harris, giving support to the Irish rugby team. His breakthrough in films came with his starring role as a rugby player in *This Sporting Life* (1963).

Film actor and director, Kenneth Brannagh, was born in Belfast.

Film star, Peter O'Toole was born in Galway in 1934.

Neil Jordan, one of Ireland's leading film directors (*Mona Lisa, Company of Wolves, The Crying Game*).

QUESTION 151

What colour is generally regarded as the national colour of Ireland?
Is it   (a) blue?
       (b) gold?
       (c) green?

QUESTION 152

How many Irish people live in urban areas (in places of 1,500 inhabitants or more) as opposed to rural?
Is it   (a) five out of ten?
       (b) six out of ten?
       (c) seven out of ten?

QUESTION 153

Anagram: S S U T I N O N I
A name for the loyalists of Northern Ireland

QUESTION 154

Who said, "*Of all the countries in the world, Ireland possesses the most varied and beautiful folk music* "?
Was it   (a) Arnold Bax (1883-1953), who held the position of Master of the King's Music (an honorary court title in Britain, dating from the reign of Charles I), a self-confessed "brazen Romantic"?
       (b) Aaron Copland (1900-90), the American composer who in some of his work displays American idioms grafted on to European tradition?
       (c) Zoltán Kodály (1882-1967), the brilliant Hungarian composer who devoted his services to his country's folk music?

ANSWER 151

(c) green. When President John F. Kennedy (1917-63) visited Ireland in 1963, he referred in his arrival speech to "this green and misty island". It is hardly surprising that a country which has, as the popular song puts it, "forty shades of green" should have adopted that colour. Green is one of the colours of the national flag; it is the colour of the uniforms of the Defence Forces. It is the colour sported by Ireland's athletes in international competitions.

We cannot say when green was first so used. There is evidence that the great military leader, Owen Roe O'Neill (1590-1649), used a green flag with a harp on it as the national flag in 1642. Certainly by 1798 green was generally accepted as the national colour. In the Rebellion of that year it appeared everywhere—in uniforms, in ribbons on hats, in flags. From then on, it embodied Ireland's assertion of its separateness from Britain.

ANSWER 152

(b) six out of ten. Up to the 1960s most people lived in rural areas.

ANSWER 153

Unionists. Until 1800 Ireland existed as a separate political entity. In that year the Act of Union abolished the Irish parliament and transferred its statutory powers to the parliament in Westminster. However, the separate Irish administrative system, based in Dublin Castle, was maintained. Throughout the nineteenth century, and into the first two decades of the twentieth century, nationalists, both constitutionalists and proponents of physical force, made a series of efforts to roll back the Union. This process culminated in the Anglo-Irish Agreement of 1921, which gave political freedom to Ireland except for six of the northern counties, as nationalists view it. The majority of the people in that area, predominantly Presbyterians and members of the Church of Ireland (Anglicans), wished to maintain the union with Britain. They are known as Unionists.

The Unionists generally regard themselves as both Irish and British. They regard the British Government of Ireland Act, which established "Northern Ireland", as the basis of *their* freedom. They have three major concerns about the reunification of Ireland, which is desired by nationalists. They fear they would lose their British identity. They fear their civic freedoms would be curtailed. They fear they would lose the social and economic benefits they derive from their link with Britain.

ANSWER 154

(a) Arnold Bax

QUESTION 155

Does the word "malapropism" mean
- (a) a circus tent pole?
- (b) a support for apple trees?
- (c) the misuse of a word by confusing it with another resembling it in sound?

QUESTION 156

The Celtic Cross is distinguished by the ring that connects the upright and the transverse of the cross. Celtic Crosses or—as they are more commonly called in Ireland—High Crosses (some are over four metres in height), along with round towers, were notable features of Irish monasteries. During the course of the nineteenth century, the Celtic Cross came to symbolise Ireland in the same way as the Cross of Lorraine symbolises France and the Maltese Cross Malta.
The Celtic Crosses come from which period?
Is it the
- (a) fifth century?
- (b) ninth century?
- (c) twelfth century?

QUESTION 157

What British writer said, "*The Irish are a fair race—they never speak well of one another*"?
Was it
- (a) Samuel Johnson (1709-84)?
- (b) Alfred Lord Tennyson (1809-92)?
- (c) William Makepeace Thackeray (1811-63)?

QUESTION 158

Three countries have won the Eurovision Song Contest five times (to 1993)—the most times it has been won by any one country.
Are they
- (a) Ireland, United Kingdom and Germany?
- (b) Ireland, United Kingdom and Italy?
- (c) Ireland, France and Luxembourg?

ANSWER 155

(c) the misuse of a word by confusing it with another resembling it in sound, usually with comical effect, as in Seán O'Casey's famous line in *Juno and the Paycock*, "The whole world's in a state of chassis". The word comes from Mrs Malaprop, a character in *The Rivals* by the Dublin-born playwright and impresario, Richard Brinsley Sheridan (1751-1816)—"She's as headstrong as an allegory on the banks of the Nile". Such errors were not uncommon in the Dublin of Sheridan's youth, when uneducated Irish speakers were trying to pick up a knowledge of English. A notable malapropism in the Dublin argot of those days was "vermin jelly", used for "vermicelli", a form of pasta then popular in the preparation of soups.

ANSWER 156

(b) and (c), both the ninth and twelfth centuries. At a bend in the River Shannon below Athlone, the geographical centre of Ireland marked by a pillar in Hodson's Bay on Lough Ree, is to be found one of the great archaeological sites in Ireland—the monastic settlement of Clonmacnois. Among the ruins stands a Celtic Cross. There are over 150 such crosses—some surviving only in part—to be found throughout Ireland. Most of the crosses in Leinster and Ulster were carved in the ninth century; those in Connacht and Munster were carved in the twelfth century. It is likely that a High Cross stood at the entrance to a monastery or at its centre, a compelling attraction in colour, for, like Greek statuary, the crosses were painted. Carved panels on the crosses depict scenes mostly from the Bible and were literally sermons in stone. No one knows for certain how the ring motif originated. Some scholars associate the ring with sun-worship: in this perspective the Celtic Crosses represent the triumph of Christianity over the old pagan religion of the druids. The Celtic Crosses are among the finest achievements of Irish art; they are among Europe's finest stone carvings in the first millennium after Christ; because of both their antiquity and subtlety, they have a place among the world's treasures in stone.

ANSWER 157

(a) Samuel Johnson (as quoted in Boswell's *Life*). Thackeray, who visited Ireland in 1842, used Ireland for the setting of his first novel *The Luck of Barry Lyndon*. Stanley Kubrick's *Barry Lyndon* (1975) is a film adaptation of that novel.

ANSWER 158

(c) Ireland, France and Luxembourg

QUESTION 159

The 1991 census in Britain shows that over a million people live in households the head of which was born in Ireland. It also shows that over 800,000 Irish-born people live in Britain. Irish immigrants to Britain have traditionally concentrated in the cities of Glasgow, Liverpool, Manchester, Leeds, Birmingham and London. The number of people of Irish descent in Britain is substantial.

Is it   (a) three million?
          (b) six million?
          (c) nine million?

QUESTION 160

Anagram: K H B O S I
Don't let them put this on you!

QUESTION 161

Which Irish poet wrote:

O body swayed to music, O brightening glance,
How can we know the dancer from the dance?

Was it   (a) Seamus Heaney?
          (b) WB Yeats?
          (c) Thomas Kinsella?

QUESTION 162

Croagh Patrick in Co. Mayo and Lough Derg ("St Patrick's Purgatory") in Co. Donegal attract thousands of pilgrims each year. However, the most popular pilgrimage in Ireland is to Knock, Co. Mayo, where the Blessed Virgin is reported to have appeared to some people over a hundred years ago. How many visits do pilgrims make to Knock each year?

Is it   (a) 500,000?
          (b) 750,000?
          (c) 1,500,000?

ANSWER 159

(b) six million, almost one in nine of the total population of Britain, according to estimates (the figure is not captured in the census).

ANSWER 160

kibosh. Great numbers of the Irish who flooded into America to escape the Famine spoke their native language, Irish. "Kibosh" is said to be the way the New York Poles rendered the Irish expression *caidhp bháis* (the death-cap), which they heard their Irish neighbours using. "To put the kibosh" on something is to give it a mortal blow, for before the burial of an uncoffined Famine victim the relatives covered the face of the dead person with a cloth—a *caidhp bháis.*

ANSWER 161

(b) WB Yeats, in "Among School Children". Ireland has a rich traditional dance culture whose development is one of the aims of the internationally renowned corps of Siamsa Tíre, the National Folk Theatre of Ireland, in Tralee, Co. Kerry.

ANSWER 162

(c) 1,500,000. The number of pilgrims is somewhat smaller because some pilgrims make a number of visits during the year. The most popular pilgrimage abroad for Irish people is to the great Marian shrine in Lourdes in the south of France, famous for its miraculous cures. The story is told of a Dublin businessman who accompanied his wife there, albeit reluctantly. One afternoon he sought solitude at the grotto, deserted because of the heat of the day. He surveyed, somewhat sceptically, the crutches of the cured festooning the shrine before flopping down dog-tired into one of the wheelchairs used for the sick. He promptly fell asleep. Some time later he was aroused by the sound of a crowd approaching. He looked up and saw a group of Italians led by a voluble friar. The Dubliner decided to make a quick departure and stood up suddenly out of the wheelchair. The friar, seeing this, clapped his hands together and exclaimed, *"Miraculo! Miraculo!"* and led his pilgrims in a rush towards the man that sent him flying among the wheelchairs. The man broke his leg in several places and had to be flown home to Dublin on a stretcher.

QUESTION 163

Early peoples, everywhere, played ball games. There were two main types, one played by propelling the ball with a stick, the other by simply handling or kicking the ball. Hockey, cricket and golf belong to the first category; rugby, soccer and Australian rules football to the latter. Ireland has two traditional ball games, one belonging to each type, namely hurling and Gaelic football. Both games are of great antiquity, the earliest reference to hurling being to a fierce hurling match, which, according to legend, preceded the battle of Moytura, in Co. Sligo, allegedly fought about 2000 BC. The mythical Ulster hero Cúchulainn was unsurpassed at hurling. Following the Famine of the 1840s the games experienced serious decline and had disappeared altogether in many areas until rescued by Michael Cusack, a teacher from Co. Clare. His new organisation, the Gaelic Athletic Association, "swept the country like a prairie fire", he wrote a few years later.

The association has since experienced extraordinary success. Today, its headquarters are at Croke Park, Dublin, the largest sports stadium in Ireland, and it possesses many fine grounds throughout the country. It is also one of the largest amateur sports organisations anywhere, with about 2,800 affiliated clubs. Of these, 2,500 are in Ireland, which is equivalent to one club for every 2,000 people in the entire country, north and south. (With the notable exception of soccer, sport in Ireland is generally organised on an island-wide basis.) Apart from founding the GAA, Cusack has another claim to fame: James Joyce used him as the model for "the Citizen" in *Ulysses*. Among those who met in Thurles, Co. Tipperary, to found the organisation was JK Bracken, a sculptor, who was the father of Brendan Bracken, head of the *Financial Times* group of newspapers, a close friend of Winston Churchill and Minister for Information in his war-time government. In what year was the GAA founded?

Was it in   (a) 1872?
           (b) 1884?
           (c) 1893?

QUESTION 164

Does the word "quark" mean
    (a) a goblet?
    (b) the call of the bittern?
    (c) a sub-atomic particle?

QUESTION 165

This is the name of an illegal Irish nationalist paramilitary organisation: the Irish _____ Army (IRA).
What is the missing word?

ANSWER 163

(b) 1884

ANSWER 164

(c) a sub-atomic particle. In their exploration of the constituents of matter, nuclear physicists have had to develop a whole new nomenclature. The central part of the atom—the nucleus—is composed of protons and neutrons. The basic constituents of protons and neutrons are quarks; three quarks make a nucleon, i.e. a proton or neutron. It was the American physicist Murray Gell-Mann who came up with the name "quark". A Joyce enthusiast, he recalled the cry from *Finnegans Wake:* "Three quarks for Muster Mark!" Joyce's fellow-countryman, the scientist ETS Walton, contributed more substantially to nuclear physics when, along with the English physicist John Cockcroft, he developed the first nuclear particle generator in 1931—"We've split the atom! We've split the atom!" they exclaimed to startled strangers on the streets of Cambridge. In 1951 Walton and Cockcroft were jointly awarded the Nobel Prize for Physics.

ANSWER 165

Republican. When the successful Sinn Féin candidates in the General Election of 1918 met in Dublin in January 1919 as the first Dáil, they established structures of government, such as ministries and courts. As part of this process the Irish Volunteers, who had taken part in the Easter Rising, became known as the Irish Republican Army and engaged in a guerilla struggle with the British forces. When the new state came into being in 1922 with the ratification of the Anglo-Irish Agreement by the Dáil, it established its own Defence Forces which many of those in the IRA joined. Some chose to continue as an armed and illegal organisation outside the constitutional process. By the early 1960s, however, the IRA had become moribund, until revitalised by the ill-judged reaction to the peaceful Civil Rights movement in Northern Ireland in the latter part of the decade.

QUESTION 166

Spain joined the European Union in 1986. Since then Irish exports to Spain have trebled, and Spain is now Ireland's ninth most important trading partner. Spain, too, is one of the most popular holiday destinations for Irish people. In the seventeenth and eighteenth centuries, when Ireland was exposed to the rapacity of early English colonial adventurers, thousands of Irish people fled to Spain and to the Spanish Netherlands where they uniquely were accorded entitlement to Spanish citizenship from the moment of their arrival. Irish noble families were given Spanish titles (thus today, for example, the Duke of Tetuan is a descendant of a first cousin of Red Hugh O'Donnell). Both in Spain and in Ireland, there is a persistent traditional belief that Ireland's early people were the Sons of Míle (the Milesians) who set sail for Ireland over two thousand years ago from the Tower of Hercules in La Coruña, Galicia. What famous Spanish writer subscribed to this belief, "...*the Irish are Spaniards who lost their way and got stranded in the North where they do not belong*"?

Was it   (a) Antonio Machado (1875-1939)?
            (b) Miguel de Unamuno (1864-1936)?
            (c) Salvador de Madariaga (1886-1978)?

QUESTION 167

Which Irish writer has one of his characters declare, "*I go to encounter for the millionth time the reality of experience, and to forge in the smithy of my soul the uncreated conscience of my race*"?

Was it   (a) WB Yeats?
            (b) Seán O'Casey?
            (c) James Joyce?

QUESTION 168

Over the gate of which Irish town was the following prayer said to have been inscribed: "*From the ferocious O'Flaherties, O Lord, deliver us!*"?

Was it   (a) Galway?
            (b) Westport?
            (c) Limerick?

QUESTION 169

Apart from the other Celtic languages which language is most closely related to Irish?

Is it   (a) Basque?
           (b) Latin?
           (c) Sanskrit?

ANSWER 166

(c) Salvador de Madariaga, in *Portrait of Europe*

ANSWER 167

(c) James Joyce, in *A Portrait of the Artist as a Young Man*

ANSWER 168

(a) Galway. This university city—as it is now—was founded on the site of a fort built by the Norman lord Richard de Burgo in 1226, following a grant to him by the English Crown. The name Galway (*Gaillimh* in Irish) means "foreign place", and for many centuries it was so regarded by the surrounding Irish, including the O'Flaherties. It survived, like an isolated Hanseatic city, by maintaining its sea links with other ports and particularly through its trade with Spain. Tradition has it that Christopher Columbus heard Mass in the Church of St Nicholas (founded in 1320), before facing the hazards of his voyage of discovery to the New World in 1492. This church contains the tomb of James Lynch Fitzstephen, mayor of Galway in 1493, who, when no one else would do it, hanged his own son for the murder of a young Spaniard who was a guest in his home. A remnant of the old city walls, and a further reminder of the links with Spain, exists in the massive Spanish Arch on the quayside.

ANSWER 169

(b) Latin. Irish is a Celtic language and its nearest relations include Scots Gaelic and Welsh. The Celtic languages form one of the ten main divisions of a related family of languages known as the Indo-European. Latin and Sanskrit also belong to this family. Latin and its daughter languages (the Romance languages, including Italian, French, Spanish, Portuguese, Catalan and Romanian) are descended from a division of the Indo-European family known as Italic. So close were the original Celtic and Italic languages that they were once considered by some to be a single family, which they called Italo-Celtic. The Indo-European peoples are thought to have originated north of the Black Sea in Ukraine and southern Russia over five thousand years ago, whence they spread out in all directions. Their furthest advance eastwards was northern India, where they established Sanskrit; Irish represents their furthest advance westwards. Certain similarities provide evidence of the common origin of Irish and Sanskrit. "*Is mé*" means "*I am*" in Irish. "*Àsmi*" means "*I am*" in Sanskrit. Basque, a language unrelated to any other known tongue, is spoken only along the western Pyrenees, in Northern Spain and Southern France.

QUESTION 170

The North Bull Island, which skirts the north shore of Dublin Bay, is an accessible and extensive nature reserve within the city limits. It comprises 350 hectares (860 acres) and is five kilometres (over three miles) in length and one kilometre in width at its widest point. As a bird sanctuary, the area is frequented by up to 40,000 birds of over 150 species during the winter months. The island provides a rare example of an undisturbed series of habitats ranging from beach to sand dunes, dune grasslands, salt marsh and mud flats. The interpretative centre on the island, which can be approached by causeway and bridge, caters for over 20,000 visitors annually. Paradoxically, this natural amenity owes its existence to a man-made construction, popularly known as the Bull Wall, which was built early in the last century, for the purpose of deepening the entrance to Dublin port. The island emerged Aphrodite-like from the sea, fed by sand carried from the river mouth by the altered currents and deposited north of the wall. This development of the port followed from a nautical survey of Dublin Bay in 1804. What noted British admiral was involved in this survey?

Was it   (a) the unfortunate Admiral Byng, who was courtmartialled and executed for his failure to relieve the Mediterranean island of Minorca?

(b) Lord Nelson, whose pillar and statue once stood in O'Connell Street in Dublin?

(c) Admiral Bligh, who is better known as Captain Bligh of HMS *Bounty*?

QUESTION 171

This is the title of a play by an Irish author.
What is the missing word?
The Shadow of a _____ by Seán O'Casey

QUESTION 172

Anagram: W E E G A R G N N
The most famous Neolithic site in Ireland

QUESTION 173

The British aviators, JW Alcock and AW Brown, made the first Atlantic crossing in an aeroplane in 1919. Flying from America, they landed on the west coast of Ireland. Was the town they landed near:

(a) Clifden, Co. Galway?

(b) Kilrush, Co. Clare?

(c) Ballybunnion, Co. Kerry?

ANSWER 170

(c) Admiral William Bligh (1754-1817). The famous mutiny on the *Bounty* occurred fifteen years earlier, in 1789. The execution of Byng prompted Voltaire (1694-1778) to remark: "In this country [England] it is thought well to kill an admiral from time to time to encourage the others" (*Dans ce pays-ci il est bon de tuer de temps en temps un amiral pour encourager les autres*—the first use of the latter phrase).

ANSWER 171

Gunman. Seán O'Casey (1888-1964), a self-educated Dublin labourer, first sprang to fame as a dramatist when the Abbey Theatre staged *The Shadow of a Gunman* in 1923 (the run rescued the theatre from financial straits). Two more plays based on the Troubles followed, *Juno and the Paycock* and *The Plough and the Stars*. After a bitter dispute with Yeats over the Abbey's refusal to stage *The Silver Tassie*, O'Casey moved to London in 1926 and determined never to return to Ireland. He continued to write—autobiography, new forms of drama, criticism and socialist political commentary.

ANSWER 172

Newgrange. One of the oldest man-made structures in the world is to be found at a bend in the River Boyne some forty kilometres north of Dublin. Carbon-dated to the same period as the oldest pyramid in Egypt, Newgrange is about five thousand years old. It consists of a massive circular mound penetrated by a stone-lined passage which leads into a vaulted burial chamber. A remarkable feature of Newgrange is that at sunrise on 21 December, the winter solstice, the sunlight advances up the dark passage and fills the great central chamber with a cold, golden light; after about seventeen minutes it retreats down the passage like a man with a lantern—or a god—departing. Another feature of Newgrange—and of the mounds of Knowth and Dowth, that together with it form the great necropolis of Brú na Bóinne—is the vast collection of massive stones, with their numinous abstract designs, on view there. It has been calculated that Brú na Bóinne holds a quarter of all the Neolithic art of Western Europe. The people who built Newgrange were the first farmers in Ireland. The first people to live in Ireland that we have a record of were not farmers but hunters and trappers of small game and fish who set up camp at Mount Sandel near Coleraine in Northern Ireland about 8,700 years ago.

ANSWER 173

(a) Clifden, Co. Galway

QUESTION 174

Which Irishman said, *"Do not do unto others as you would they should do unto you. Their tastes may not be the same"*?

Was it   (a) George Bernard Shaw?

           (b) Hugh Leonard?

           (c) Dion Boucicault?

QUESTION 175

Anagram: C R E U N N T O
A musical form

QUESTION 176

This is the title of a play by an Irish author.
What is the missing word?
Dancing at _____ by Brian Friel

QUESTION 177

St Columbanus (543-615) was the foremost early Irish missionary to the continent of Europe. He worked in the ancient kingdom of Burgundy until Theodoric II banished him, whereupon he moved to northern Italy. The area of his activities covered parts of modern France, Germany, Italy, Switzerland and Austria. He is still honoured in those countries, in all of which his memory lives on in a variety of placenames, from Monte Colombano to Sanggeliboo (Sanct Colombano). A stone cross in the Bay of St Coulomb in Brittany marks the place where, by tradition, he first set foot on the European mainland. His work to rechristianise Europe after the collapse of the Roman Empire prompted, in our own time, a leading European statesman engaged in picking up the pieces after World War II to say of Columbanus: *"St Columbanus is the patron saint of all those who seek to build a united Europe"*.

Was he   (a) Robert Schuman (1886-1963) of France?

           (b) Konrad Adenauer (1876-1967) of Germany?

           (c) Alcide de Gasperi (1881-1954) of Italy?

ANSWER 174

(a) George Bernard Shaw, in *Man and Superman*. Dion Boucicault (*c*.1820-90), born in Dublin, was an actor and playwright with some 150 plays to his name. He wrote *The Octoroon*, the first play to treat seriously the position of black Americans; it created a sensation when produced in New York in 1859. Some of his plays, especially *The Colleen Bawn* and *The Shaughraun* (*seachrán* is "wandering", "astray" in Irish), are still performed. "Octoroon" was the name given by a racially obsessed society to a person who had one black great-grandparent.

Hugh Leonard (1927-   ) is one of Ireland's most successful contemporary playwrights. His most renowned play is probably *Da*.

ANSWER 175

nocturne. The Irish composer, John Field (1782-1837), devised the nocturne form, a short lyrical musical piece usually for the piano. He worked mainly in Russia, where he gained a high reputation as a performer and teacher. His influence on Chopin (1810-49), whose nocturnes are modelled on his, is well known. Musicologists regard his output, which was comparatively small, as containing some lyrical pieces as perfect as any written by his successors. The John Field Room in the National Concert Hall in Dublin salutes his achievements. Field is buried in Moscow.

ANSWER 176

Lughnasa. Lug ("Lugh" or "Lú" in modern Irish) was the great god of the Celts. The month of August in Irish (*Lughnasa*, or *Lúnasa* in modern Irish spelling) is named after him. Lug was probably the god of fertility, since his festival was held at the beginning of August, the commencement of the harvest. His name appears in placenames across Europe, wherever the Celts settled. Co. Louth in Ireland is named after him; so is Carlisle (originally Luguvallum) in England; Lyons (Lugudunum), Laon, Leon and Loudon in France; Leiden in the Netherlands; and Legnica (formerly Liegnitz) in Poland. In Celtic times, the festival of Lug was celebrated with games, notably at Lyons in France and, down to the early nineteenth century, at Telltown in Co. Meath (the Tailteann Games).

ANSWER 177

(a) Robert Schuman, speaking on the issue of which saint should be the patron saint of a united Europe. St Benedict (*c*.480–*c*.547), founder of the Benedictines, was eventually nominated.

Seamus Heaney, born in Derry in 1939, has attained such stature as to be compared with WB Yeats. Though technically remote from the older poet, he shares his commitment to the resuscitation of the cultural integrity of Ireland.

Eavan Boland, born in Dublin in 1944, is one of the most accomplished of Irish poets. "Nothing has ever been a greater influence on me", she has said, "than to move from the world of urbane learning ... to the quiet barbarities of the suburbs."

Desmond Egan, born in Athlone in 1936, received the National Poetry Foundation of the USA award in 1983. A widely translated poet, he has had his books published in French, Dutch, Italian, German, Danish, Swedish, and Japanese.

Roddy Doyle, born in Dublin in 1958, the hilarious chronicler of the gutsy resilience of Dublin's underprivileged. "They had absolutely nothing. But they were willing to risk it all."

Maeve Binchy, born in Dublin, is one of the most popular international bestselling authors (*Light a Penny Candle, Firefly Summer, Circle of Friends, The Lilac Bus*).

Michael Longley, born in Belfast in 1939, is one of the leading Northern poets and has produced, in the view of critics, some of the most memorable poems about the Troubles in Northern Ireland.

Paul Durcan, born in Dublin in 1944, has achieved cult status by turning poetry once more into a popular performance art. His work brings laughter to social insecurities and pathos to quotidian certainties.

Brendan Kennelly, born in Kerry in 1936, is professor of modern literature in Trinity College, Dublin, and one of the most prolific and most popular of contemporary Irish poets. He sees poetry "basically as a celebration of human inadequacy and failure".

A woodcut from *Sankt Brandans Seefahrt*, a German version of the *Navigatio Brendani* ('St Brendan's Voyage'), printed in Augsburg in 1476. The big fish represents a whale. It refers to a famous incident in the account of the sixth-century Irish monk's Atlantic explorations. Fifteen days out from Ireland the monks made landfall on a small and completely bare island. They lit a fire to prepare a meal. As the cauldron began to boil the island began to move. The startled monks scrambled back into their leather-covered boat; the island swam rapidly away.

The Celtic Cross at Monasterboice, Co. Louth, the finest surviving example. Standing in the open, exposed to the elements, the crosses no longer exhibit any traces of the paint that originally covered them. Scholars conclude they were painted because some of the intertwined designs can be understood only if they are picked out in different colours. Moreover we know from the surviving illuminated manuscripts that the monasteries commanded the skills of superb colourists.

The early Christian monastery on Skellig Michael. The stone beehive huts were individual cells for the monks.

QUESTION 178

Which modern armament was pioneered by an Irishman?
Was it   (a) the tank?
         (b) the submarine?
         (c) the air-to-air missile?

QUESTION 179

A foreign observer of the Irish said, "*It is in the cultivation of instrumental music I consider the proficiency of this people to be worthy of commendation; and in this their skill is beyond all comparison, beyond that of any nation I have seen*".

Was it   (a) Prince HLV Pückler-Muskau, in the course of his *Tour in England, Ireland, and France in the years 1828 and 1829*?
        (b) Don Francisco de Cuellar, captain of the Spanish Armada galleon *San Pedro*, who was shipwrecked on Streedagh Strand, Co. Sligo, in 1588, and who wrote an account of his adventures in Ireland and Scotland after his escape to the Spanish Netherlands?
        (c) Giraldus Cambrensis (Gerald the Welshman), the literary name of Geraldus de Barri (*c.*1146-1243), who visited Ireland in the twelfth century?

QUESTION 180

This is the name of a play by an Irish author.
What is the missing word?
John Bull's Other _____ by George Bernard Shaw

QUESTION 181

Which Celtic scholar said, "*In nature poetry the Gaelic muse may vie with that of any other nation. Indeed, these poems occupy a unique position in the literature of the world. To seek out and watch and love Nature, in its tiniest phenomena as in its grandest, was given to no other people so early and so fully as to the Celt. Many hundreds of Gaelic and Welsh poems testify to this fact* "?
Was it   (a) Holger Pedersen of Denmark?
        (b) Georges Dottin of France?
        (c) Kuno Meyer of Germany?

ANSWER 178

(b) the submarine. John Holland (1841-1914), an ardent Irish patriot born in Liscannor, Co. Clare, where there is a memorial to him, emigrated to America. There in 1881, he designed and built the *Fenian Ram*, the prototype of the modern submarine, to attack British warships. His later models were bought by the US navy.

ANSWER 179

(c) Giraldus Cambrensis, in the chronicle of his visit, *Topographica Hiberniae*. The musical instrument associated with Ireland from earliest times is the harp, so much so that it is the premier national symbol. The harp was introduced to Irish coinage by the English King Henry VIII. On these coins, the Crown, the symbol of the English monarchy, surmounted the harp. "The harp without the crown" came to epitomise the demand of Irish republicans. A story from the late nineteenth century tells of an Irish-American who was brought before a police magistrate on the flimsy grounds of "harbouring seditious designs". One of the points produced in evidence against him was that he was wearing a "Republican hat". When defending counsel asked what that might be, the magistrate caustically interposed, "I presume it is a hat without a crown". The harp, without the crown, is now the official logo of the Irish government and it appears on all Irish coins.

ANSWER 180

Island. In this play, Shaw sought to dramatise the differences between the Irish and English temperaments, to break down the romantic conception of the Irish held by the English, and to destroy the stereotype of the stage Irish. When at a command performance on 11 March 1905, Edward VII laughed with such gusto that the chair beneath him broke, Shaw's reputation soared and *John Bull's Other Island* played to continual laughter and applause at succeeding performances.

ANSWER 181

(c) Kuno Meyer (1858-1919), who lectured in German in Liverpool University, in *Selections from Ancient Irish Poetry* (1911). Kuno Meyer devoted himself to what he called the "fascinating study of the vernacular literature of ancient Ireland, the earliest voice from the dawn of West European civilisation".

QUESTION 182

Anagram: M Y T H N U A I
It's all of what we are

QUESTION 183

Douglas Hyde (1860-1949), a brilliant language scholar and first President of
Ireland, wrote, "In most countries the Devil is the great outstanding
anthropomorphic conception added to the folklore of Europe by the
introduction of Christianity; and later the belief in witches, who trafficked
directly with the Evil One, became extraordinarily prevalent and powerful.
Now the most striking fact about Irish legends of saints and sinners is that the
Devil personified rarely appears at all, and witches never. The belief in witches,
and in witches' sabbaths, with which other nations were positively obsessed,
and which gave rise to such hecatombs of unhappy victims in almost all the
Protestant, and in some of the Catholic, countries in Europe, as well as in
America, never found its way into native Ireland at all, or disturbed Gaelic
sanity, although a few isolated instances occurred among the English settlers".

The most celebrated of these rare instances was the trial of Dame Alice
Kyteler in Kilkenny, then ruled by the Ormondes (of Norman descent). Alice
was accused of sacrificing "nine red cocks and nine peacocks' eies" to a spirit
called Robert Artisson. Her unfortunate maidservant, Petronilla, was burnt at
the stake, but Dame Alice herself escaped to obscurity in England. Her house,
the oldest in Kilkenny, has been restored and reopened as Kyteler's Inn. When
did her trial take place?

Was it in   (a) 1324?
          (b) 1469?
          (c) 1540 ?

QUESTION 184

In 1990, the total amount of tax collected by the government in the Republic,
expressed as a percentage of gross domestic product (the value of the goods
and services produced in the state in the year) was 37.6%. In one of the
following countries the percentage was less.

Was it   (a) Denmark?
      (b) Spain?
      (c) Netherlands?

QUESTION 185

Charles Bianconi (1786-1875) from Lombardy in Italy became famous in Ireland.

Was he   (a) a printer of popular ballads and songs?
      (b) a temperance preacher?
      (c) an entrepreneur?

ANSWER 182

humanity. In 1822, Richard Martin (1754-1834) succeeded in getting through the Westminster parliament the first Act to be passed anywhere for the protection of animals. A wealthy Galway landlord, he was so generally benevolent that he was nicknamed "Humanity Dick". While Martin was largely concerned with the welfare of common animals, a contemporary of his in Co. Mayo, George Robert Fitzgerald ("Fighting Fitzgerald"), was concerned for a species rare for Ireland—he kept a pet bear which he treated as a boon companion and took with him everywhere. Once, Fitzgerald's lawyer, travelling through the night with him in his carriage, discovered when dawn broke that the "gentleman" beside him, swathed in a blue travelling cloak, had a face covered in fur and a big red tongue lolling over fearsome teeth. When, upon Fitzgerald's command, the bear kissed the solicitor, the poor fellow leapt from the carriage and dashed for safety.

ANSWER 183

(a) about 1324. Interestingly, there is no word in Irish for "witch". One of the most notorious witch trials took place in Salem, Massachusetts, towards the end of the seventeenth century: nineteen women were put to death there on charges of witchcraft. Among these was Anne Glover, an Irishwoman who had been transported by the Cromwellians to Barbados and later brought to Salem as a house-servant. She could respond to her interrogators only in her native Irish. They seized upon this as evidence of discourse with the Devil.

ANSWER 184

(b) Spain (34.4%). In Denmark the figure was 49.9%, in the Netherlands 46%. Because the dependency ratio in the Republic is exceptionally high—every ten people at work must support 22 other people (children, the sick and handicapped, the unemployed and the retired)—the tax burden on each person at work is relatively high.

ANSWER 185

(c) an entrepreneur. At the beginning of the nineteenth century there had been a considerable improvement in the road system in Ireland. After the Napoleonic Wars there was a surplus of horses and vehicles. Bianconi related these facts to establish in 1815 a road passenger service between Cahir and Clonmel. Within a few short years his "long cars" were a familiar sight in Munster and the West. He served the travelling public until the railways took over in the middle of the century, when he retired a wealthy man.

QUESTION 186

Through its art, particularly its literature, Ireland has carried out some of the most brilliant and original explorations of the human consciousness. But while Ireland is now experiencing one of its recurrent periods of artistic resurgence, it is probable that its strongest claim to sensibility and humaneness is being made by the sustained endeavours of some five thousand missionaries and relief workers, both Catholic and Protestant (though predominantly Catholic), in eighty-five countries throughout the world. These volunteers are bringing education, health and development services to some of the poorest people on earth. In doing so, they share the indignities of life in the *favelas* of Brazil, they face down the threats of sugar barons in the Philippines, they endure the heart-breaking loneliness of sundown in the African bush. The majority is indeed in Africa, in thirty-three countries (in the Latin American-Caribbean region they are in twenty-four countries, in Asia-Oceania they are in twenty-four countries, and in the Middle East they are in four countries). Which African country has the biggest concentration of Irish missionaries?

        Is it   (a) South Africa?
                (b) Kenya?
                (c) Nigeria?

QUESTION 187

Who described the design of coinage as *"the silent ambassadors of national taste"*?

        Was it   (a) Michael Collins (1890-1922), the leader of the armed struggle against the British and the first Irish Minister for Finance?
                (b) William Butler Yeats (1869-1939), poet and dramatist ?
                (c) Sam Stephenson, the modern architect who has left his mark on Ireland's capital with such buildings as the Central Bank and Dublin's Civic Offices?

QUESTION 188

Patrick Kavanagh (1905-67), who was born on a small farm in Co. Monaghan, is one of the most important Irish poets of the twentieth century. In one of his sonnets, "Epic", he vividly describes a local squabble over boundaries between neighbouring farmers. He was inclined to dismiss the episode as trivial until it occurred to him to compare it to the subject of another well-known literary work.

        Was this   (a) Homer's *Iliad* ?
                 (b) Rabelais's *Gargantua and Pantagruel* ?
                 (c) Shakespeare's *King Lear*?

ANSWER 186

(a) South Africa, with 18% of the total. The five thousand represent one out of every thousand of the population of Ireland. A comparable effort by Britain would require 55,000 volunteers and by the USA 250,000.

ANSWER 187

(b) William Butler Yeats. In 1926 Yeats, then a member of the Irish Senate, chaired a committee to advise the government on the design of a distinctive Irish silver and copper coinage. The committee recommended that all coins should have a harp, the great national symbol, on one side, and a particular bird or beast on the other side, depending on the denomination. "We asked advice as to the symbols", Yeats said, "and were recommended by the public: round towers, wolfhounds, shamrocks... and advised by the Society of Antiquaries to avoid patriotic emblems altogether... If we decided on birds and beasts, the artist—as the experience of centuries has shown—might achieve a masterpiece, and might, so it seemed to us, please those who would look longer at each coin than anybody else—artists and children. Besides, what better symbols could we find for this horse-riding, salmon-fishing, cattle-raising country?" So, in 1928, Ireland became the first modern state to design and issue an entire coinage. The competition for the design was won by an English artist, Percy Metcalfe, who also designed the first real British commemorative coin, a silver crown, struck to mark the jubilee of George V in 1935.

ANSWER 188

(a) the *Iliad*. Kavanagh says:

> *... I inclined*
> *To lose my faith in Ballyrush and Gortin*
> *Till Homer's ghost came whispering to my mind;*
> *He said: I made the Iliad from such*
> *A local row.*

QUESTION 189

The Irish, as Salvador de Madariaga observed in *Englishmen, Frenchmen and Spaniards*, cannot resist giving the English a dig. Oscar Wilde gave one of the wickedest with this characterisation of *Burke's Peerage*, the great genealogical record of the English establishment: "*You should study the Peerage, Gerald... It is the best thing in fiction the English have ever done*". In which of his works do these lines occur?

Is it in   (a) *A Woman of No Importance*?
                   (b) *The Picture of Dorian Gray*?
                   (c) *An Ideal Husband*?

QUESTION 190

When did Ireland join the European Union?

Was it in   (a) 1957?
                (b) 1973?
                (c) 1981?

QUESTION 191

The sea which divides Ireland from Britain is 320 km at its widest. What is it at its narrowest?

Is it   (a) 17.6 km?
            (b) 27.6 km?
            (c) 37.6 km?

QUESTION 192

In which of his plays did Shaw write, "*We have no more right to consume happiness without producing it than to consume wealth without producing it* "?

Was it   (a) *Candida*?
            (b) *Man and Superman*?
            (c) *Mrs Warren's Profession*?

QUESTION 193

Anagram: S C H R O K M A
What to wear on St Patrick's Day?

ANSWER 189

(a) *A Woman of No Importance*

ANSWER 190

(b) 1973, along with Denmark and the United Kingdom. Greece joined in 1981, Portugal and Spain in 1986, and the former East Germany in 1990. Ireland, of course, has long and close ties with the United Kingdom but within the EU she also relates closely to France on agricultural policy in particular, and to Greece, Portugal, Southern Italy (the Mezzogiorno) and Spain—the peripheral countries—on regional policy. Ireland is a major financial beneficiary of the Union. The EU was founded in 1957 when six countries, Belgium, France, Germany, Italy, Luxembourg, and the Netherlands, signed the Treaty of Rome.

ANSWER 191

(a) 17.6 km, where it divides Northern Ireland from Scotland

ANSWER 192

(a) *Candida*

ANSWER 193

shamrock. The three-leafed shamrock, one of the national symbols of Ireland, first appears by name in English in 1571; the Irish form of the word, *seamróg* (a diminutive of *seamair* "clover") is not found in written Irish until much later, 1707. However, legend has it that St Patrick employed the shamrock to explain the doctrine of the Holy Trinity—that there are three persons in one God—to the High King Laoghaire at Tara. The plant generally sported on St Patrick's Day (17 March) is one of either of two forms of clover, the Lesser Trefoil or White Clover, which, worn before they flower, are entirely green.

The first reference to the shamrock as a badge (in 1681) is quite late. However, the clover was also the emblem of Hanover, a fact which no doubt made the shamrock quite acceptable to the Irish Ascendancy as a symbol when George Louis, Duke of Brunswick-Lüneburg, or Hanover, succeeded to the English throne as George I in 1714. Irish uniformed personnel are permitted to wear the shamrock on St Patrick's Day, and in Britain an attempt is still made to meld the two traditions by having a member of the Royal Family present shamrock to the Irish Guards regiment of the British Army. The four-leafed shamrock, or clover, is believed to bring luck, being related to an earlier sign enclosed in a circle (the sun or wheel symbol) designed to ward off evil.

QUESTION 194

Three-quarters of the world population of the Greenland Whitefronted Goose—the rarest goose in Europe—winter in Ireland. The Irish government has established a wildlife reserve for them in which one of the following counties: (a) Waterford?
(b) Wexford?
(c) Wicklow?

QUESTION 195

Anagram: Y A N T M A M
Hall of Fame?

QUESTION 196

Which British eighteenth-century traveller in Ireland wrote about the Protestant Ascendancy and their Catholic tenants, *"A landlord in Ireland can scarcely invent an order which a servant, a labourer, or cottar dares to refuse to execute... Disrespect or anything tending towards sauciness he may punish with his cane or his horsewhip with the most perfect security"*?
Was it   (a) Arthur Young (1741-1820) in *A Tour in Ireland*?
(b) Richard Twiss (1747-1821) in *A Tour in Ireland in 1775*?
(c) John Bush in *Hibernia Curiosa* (1764)?

QUESTION 197

In order to increase employment, the Republic has a sophisticated programme of incentives, including a ten per cent rate of tax on profits until 2010, to attract overseas investment in manufacturing industry. Of the total number at work, 1,125,000, manufacturing industry employs 20% (225,000). Of this 225,000, 44% (99,000) are employed in almost 1,000 foreign-owned factories. The USA, UK and Germany are by far the biggest investors, in that order. How many people are employed (1993) in US-owned factories?
Is it   (a) 26,000?
(b) 44,000?
(c) 51,000?

QUESTION 198

Ireland's greatest length from north to south is 486 km. What is its greatest width (from east to west)?
Is it   (a) 225 km?
(b) 250 km?
(c) 275 km?

Answer 194

(b) Wexford, in the sunny south-east of the country

Answer 195

Tammany. In the 1990 US census almost 40 million people (15 per cent of the population) claimed Irish descent. Over half of these are Protestant, in the main descendants of the Ulster Presbyterians whose exodus to the North American colonies began in 1718, when their leases in Ireland ran out and their rents were raised beyond their capacity or willingness to pay. They called themselves Irish but were later called Scots-Irish (since the ancestors of many of them originally came from Scotland) to distinguish them from the refugees from the Irish Famine of the 1840s. The latter were mainly Catholics, most of whom settled in the large cities of America from the middle of the nineteenth century onwards. Both traditions have made exceptional contributions to American politics. Thus, four of the signatories of the American Constitution/Declaration of Independence were of Irish extraction, thirteen US Presidents were of Scots-Irish descent and two (John F. Kennedy and Ronald Reagan) were of Irish Catholic extraction.

But the Irish contributed to the dark side of American politics too. Thus, between 1870 and 1950, they controlled New York City through the powerful Democratic political organisation based in Tammany Hall, which their activities turned into a by-word for political corruption. The culture of Tammany Hall was caught nicely by Boss Croker (born in Co. Cork in 1841) when he defined an honest man as someone who, when he's bought, stays bought. The last Irish-born mayor of New York, William O'Dwyer, from Bohola, Co. Mayo, resigned in 1950. Tammany ceased to exist as a political machine after 1965.

Answer 196

(a) Arthur Young. His survey *Travels in France* (1792) was in great demand in England because of its portrait of France on the eve of the revolution; the Convention had it translated into French and published in Paris in 1793 as an indictment of the *ancien régime*.

Answer 197

(b) 44,000, in almost 400 factories that include Intel, Microsoft, Fruit of the Loom.

Answer 198

(c) 275 km

QUESTION 199

RTE's Late Late Show, hosted by Gay Byrne, is the longest running television chat show in the world. When did it start?

Was it in   (a) 1960?
              (b) 1961?
              (c) 1962?

QUESTION 200

What politician of Irish descent once described an opponent as "*a shiver looking for a spine to run up*"?

Was it   (a) Mayor Daly of Chicago?
          (b) US Senator Joe McCarthy?
          (c) Paul Keating, prime minister of Australia?

QUESTION 201

In 1685, following the revocation of the Edict of Nantes, 600,000 French Protestants became displaced persons, seeking refuge in Switzerland, the Netherlands, Britain, Germany, Russia, America and Ireland. How many of these Huguenots, as they were known, settled in Ireland?

Was it   (a) 3,000?
          (b) 10,000?
          (c) 13,000?

QUESTION 202

The average air temperatures for the coldest months in Ireland, January and February, range from 4° to 7° Celsius. What is the warmest period of the year in Ireland?

Is it   (a) May and June?
          (b) June and July?
          (c) July and August?

QUESTION 203

Anagram: C H A P N E L E U R
An elusive gentleman with a golden hoard

ANSWER 199

(b) 1961

ANSWER 200

(c) Paul Keating

ANSWER 201

(b) 10,000. Including Dublin, twenty-three settlements of Huguenots were established throughout Ireland, from Cork to Belfast. Their religious services in French ceased only when the post of French pastor in Portarlington, Co. Laois, was terminated in 1841. George Bernard Shaw derived the names of characters in *The Doctor's Dilemma* and *The Devil's Disciple* from inscriptions on the tombstones in the Huguenot cemetery which is preserved beside St Stephen's Green in Dublin. Joyce's *Finnegans Wake* also has many allusions to Huguenot names. Huguenot surnames still flourish in Ireland—La Touche, de Foubert, Fleury, Vignoles, and Blanc are examples.

ANSWER 202

(c) July and August, with average temperatures of about 15° Celsius, rising occasionally to 25°. The sunniest period is in May and June when most of the country can expect to have an average of between 5.5 and 6.5 hours of sunshine per day.

ANSWER 203

leprechaun. In the early 1950s, before he began production on his film *Darby O'Gill and the Little People,* Walt Disney, whose surname derived from Huguenots (D'Isney) who settled in Co. Cork in the seventeenth century, came to Ireland: he wanted to meet a leprechaun and have a chat with him. He did not succeed in his mission but he did get people to talk about his movie. Those who have seen a leprechaun describe him as a little man hardly more than six inches tall, dressed in green and wearing a tall hat with a feather in it. Every leprechaun has a crock of gold. If you can catch hold of one, you can force him to give you his gold. If you take your eye off him for a moment, though, he vanishes into thin air. Leprechauns, alas, are adept at distracting ordinary people. The word "leprechaun" comes from the Irish *lúchorpán*, from *lú* (smallest) and *corpán* (body), and derives from the practice of the Christian monks of retaining the charm of the old pagan stories by turning the gods into harmless "little people".

QUESTION 204

Anagram: N D E C I M I E
Matters of life or death?

QUESTION 205

About 12km off the coast of Kerry, a volcanic rock called Skellig Michael rises 250 metres out of the Atlantic. On its summit, and almost perfectly preserved, is a small early Christian monastery. Dedicated to St Michael the Archangel, it recalls the similarly sited and similarly dedicated Mont-Saint-Michel in Brittany, France. Beside it is a smaller island, the Lesser Skellig, preserved by the Irish government as a bird sanctuary. On it nest the second biggest concentration of gannets in Western Europe. They number how many nesting pairs?

        Is it   (a) 13,000?
               (b) 23,000?
               (c) 33,000?

QUESTION 206

This is the title of a book about a pair of well-known Irish "characters".
What is the missing word?
The Tailor and _____ by Eric Cross

QUESTION 207

A writer with an Irish father and a Greek mother was the pivotal figure in introducing Japanese studies to the Western world and in promoting Western literature in Japan.

        Was he   (a) Dion Boucicault?
                (b) Patricio Lafcadio Hearn?
                (c) John Boyle O'Reilly?

ANSWER 204

medicine. William Stokes (1804-78) was one of the many nineteenth-century physicians of genius who established Ireland's reputation as a world medical centre. Along with John Cheyne (1777-1836), a Scot who spent most of his medical career in the Royal College of Surgeons in Dublin, he described a type of intermittent breathing which usually signals the approach of death. It is known in the medical literature as "Cheyne-Stokes respiration".

ANSWER 205

(b) 23,000. The largest concentration of gannets is on St Kilda in Scotland, with double that number. The Irish word *sceilg* (whence the name) is cognate with Scilly and Skerries; they all derive from the Norse *sker* "a small rocky island".

ANSWER 206

Ansty. Banned soon after its publication in 1942 as being "in its general tendency indecent" (under the conservative censorship regime of the time virtually every Irish writer of distinction was banned), this book captures the thoughts of a remarkable old couple who lived in a tiny cottage on the mountain road up to Gougane Barra lake in Co. Cork. Here is the Tailor's famous story in support of his view that a sow is a very intelligent animal: "I was on the road to this side of Turendubh. There is a pool there at the side of the road, and a 'johnny the bog' [a crane] had caught an eel in the pond and was swallowing him. The 'johnny the bog' is a strange kind of bird. He has only a straight gut. Well, he was swallowing the eel and he wasn't making much of a hand at the business, for the eel ran straight through him, and the 'johnny the bog' kept swallowing him and losing him again. John Jerry had a sow at that time and she was always on the side of the road. She came along and stood for a while and watched the 'johnny the bog' go through the performance several times. Then she made a grab for the eel herself and swallowed him and clapped her backside up against the wall!"

ANSWER 207

(b) Patricio Lafcadio Hearn (1850-1904). Born on the Greek island of Levkas (Leucadia in classical times, whence his unusual name), he was brought up in a number of places, including Dublin. In 1869 he went to America where he became a writer and journalist. In 1890 he was sent to Japan by an American publisher. He found the country so attractive that he decided to spend the rest of his life there. He married a Japanese lady of high Samurai rank. In 1895 he became a Japanese citizen. He wrote twelve books on aspects of Japanese culture the most influential of which was *Japan, an Attempt at Interpretation.*

QUESTION 208

Anagram: B E A R H I N I
The name the Romans gave the Emerald Isle

QUESTION 209

What Irish-American personality said, as he scanned a contract, *"The big print giveth and the small print taketh away"*?

Was it   (a) Archbishop John Fulton Sheen (1895-1979), the broadcaster and prolific author of books and pamphlets?

           (b) Bing Crosby (1904-77), ("The Old Groaner"), crooner and film star?

           (c) Eugene O'Neill (1888-1953), whose play *The Iceman Cometh* was once described as *Long Day's Journey into Night* without the laughs?

QUESTION 210

In which of his plays did Shaw write, *"All professions are conspiracies against the laity"*?

Was it   (a) *Heartbreak House*?

           (b) *The Doctor's Dilemma*?

           (c) *The Devil's Disciple*?

QUESTION 211

Jim Bolger, the prime minister of New Zealand, is of Irish extraction (his parents came from Wexford). How many of his three million fellow-countrymen share his background?

Is it   (a) one in four?

          (b) one in seven?

          (c) one in ten?

ANSWER 208

Hibernia. The Iverni were a Celtic-speaking people pushed westwards into Ireland. "Hibernia", the name the Romans gave Ireland, is believed to be a corruption of Ivernia—the land of the Iverni. (They were the dominant people of Munster. Ptolemy, the second-century AD Greco-Egyptian geographer and astronomer, records their existence.) So, too, is the old Greek word for Ireland, *Ierne*. *Éire*, which is the name for Ireland in the Irish language, also appears to derive from the same source. "Erin" is an anglicisation of *Éirinn*, a form of *Éire*. "Hibernia" survives most frequently in its adjectival form "Hibernian".

ANSWER 209

(a) Archbishop John Fulton Sheen. Of all graphic forms, roman type, as printed in newspapers and books, including this book, is probably the most common in the world today. Roman type uses two kinds of lettering in the normal sentence—upper case (capital letters) and lower case (letters whose normal height is somewhat more than half that of the capitals, though some like b and d have ascenders and others like p and y have descenders, which increase their height or depth).

The lower case modern roman type is partly derived from the script developed by Irish monks in the fifth century, who used what is called the Irish half-uncial (uncial means "inch long") style. This style was characterised by well-rounded forms with, in distinction to the capital forms, ascenders and descenders. These, however, were kept so short as to contain the letters that had either feature within the body height of the other letters. As the influence of Irish monks and scholars spread through western Europe so did their style of writing. The Carolingian style, which Charlemagne promoted, was influenced by the Irish half-uncial. It in turn was the model for the lower-case type developed in northern Italy during the Renaissance.

There is an historical *justesse* in the fact that the influence of Ireland, which had done so much for European enlightenment during the Dark Ages, is still conveyed by possibly the greatest vehicle for learning ever created—the printing press.

ANSWER 210

(c) *The Devil's Disciple*

ANSWER 211

(b) one in seven (fourteen per cent), although some estimates place it as high as sixteen per cent. Mr Bolger is the fourth New Zealand prime minister of Irish stock. In 1893 New Zealand, under the premiership of Antrim-born John Ballance, became the first country to give the vote to women.

QUESTION 212

Anagram: U N F O L D W H O
A large dog

QUESTION 213

Sir Alfred Chester Beatty (1875-1968), born in New York of part-Irish descent, assembled one of the greatest and most precious collections of oriental books and manuscripts in the world. He came to reside in Ireland in 1953, where he had his collection housed in a specially constructed building. The Chester Beatty Library, which he subsequently bequeathed to the Irish people, contains 13,000 volumes and other valuable material, including Babylonian clay tablets dating back to 2500 BC.
Is this library, which is open to the public, located in
    (a) Dublin?
    (b) Maynooth?
    (c) Waterford?

QUESTION 214

The people of Kerry are famous in Ireland for their psychological subtlety and their way with words. In such a culture any departure from good grammar is socially unfortunate. Consider the situation of the Kenmare tailor whom TJ Barrington tells us about in his masterly *Discovering Kerry* audio-tapes, who many years ago needed to replace his tailor's goose. He wanted to order two of the ironing devices from his suppliers in Dublin so that he would have a spare. But what is the plural of a tailor's goose? Geese? Gooses? The tailor thought long about the problem. Finally he wrote: "Please send me one tailor's goose". But he added a postscript: "Since you are sending one goose, you might as well send two". Each year a week-long festival for writers is held in a town in Kerry.
Is the town   (a) Listowel?
    (b) Tralee?
    (c) Dingle?

QUESTION 215

The Statutes of Kilkenny were passed in which year?
Was it   (a) 1366?
    (b) 1466?
    (c) 1566?

ANSWER 212

wolfhound. The wolf was a common animal in early Ireland, and the Celtic inhabitants bred a special dog, the Irish wolfhound, to hunt it. Typically, the Irish wolfhound has a powerful body with a rough wiry coat which can be grey, fawn, red or black. The Irish wolfhound and the Great Dane are the tallest breeds of dog in existence. Both dogs can exceed a height of 99cm at the shoulder. The Irish wolfhound, which nearly suffered extinction in the nineteenth century, is one of the icons of Ireland. The Irish Guards of the British Army keep an Irish wolfhound as their mascot.

ANSWER 213

(a) Dublin

ANSWER 214

(a) Listowel. The plural of a tailor's goose is gooses.

ANSWER 215

(a) 1366. Unlike England, which was completely subdued by William the Conqueror and his Norman barons at the Battle of Hastings 1066, Ireland was never overcome by the Normans. Within a century of their arrival in 1169, they controlled two-thirds of the country. The following hundred years saw a sustained recovery of territory by the native rulers, and a continuous assimilation of the Normans who were intermarrying with Irish families. Militarily, the Irish had proved no match for the new arrivals. Culturally, they were gaining the upper hand—the Normans, as the well-known expression has it, were becoming more Irish than the Irish themselves (*"Hibernicis ipsis Hiberniores"*.) The Statutes of Kilkenny, the most famous of a series of enactments by the English Crown, sought to extirpate all Irish cultural practices, from the practice of native law to the cultivation of literature in Irish, the playing of the indigenous game of hurling and even wearing one's hair in the distinctive Irish style ("the Irish glib"). For, remarkably, all the large groups of settlers in Ireland—Danes, Normans, English, Huguenots—have been seduced by, and thoroughly absorbed into, the autochthonous culture (which they thereby further enriched)—all except, fatefully, the vast majority of the descendants of the Scots and English planters of the seventeenth century in the North of Ireland who subsist apart as today's 900,000-strong Unionist community. Kilkenny city, seat of the parliament which passed the infamous laws, is situated where the castle of the Butlers, a leading Norman family in medieval Ireland, towers over the river Nore. Anne Boleyn (1507-36), second wife of Henry VIII and mother of Elizabeth I, was a relation of the Butlers. Kilkenny, with its castle and cathedral, its winding lanes and darting alleys, is possibly the most delightful of Irish inland towns.

QUESTION 216

It was George Bernard Shaw who said England and America were two countries divided by a common language. An example of what he was talking about is the sentence "I am mad about my flat" which in British English means "I am delighted with my apartment" and in American English means "I am furious because I've got a puncture". The English spoken in Ireland is also distinctive; it owes much in its pronunciation, rhythms, structures and imagery to the substratum of Irish which still underpins everyday speech. Synge, in *The Playboy of the Western World*, captures many of these features when he has his hero, Christy Mahon, describe his crazed father as "rising up in the red dawn, or before it maybe, and going out into the yard as naked as an ash tree in the moon of May, and shying clods against the visage of the stars till he'd put the fear of death into the *banbhs* and the screeching sows". (A *banbh* is a piglet in Irish.) The locale of Synge's play is the far west of Ireland, but the verbal characteristics he employs can be found almost anywhere.

Seán O'Casey located three of his most famous plays in the back-streets of his native Dublin. In which of these plays do the following examples of Hiberno-English occur: "*They're after backing the wrong horse*" (They have backed the wrong horse) and "*She has the life frightened out of them*" (She has terrified them)?

        Is it   (a) *The Shadow of a Gunman*?
                (b) *The Plough and the Stars*?
                (c) *Juno and the Paycock*?

QUESTION 217

Dublin was a Viking city for how long?
        Was it   (a) 130 years?
                (b) 230 years?
                (c) 330 years?

QUESTION 218

Roman Catholics form 96% of the population of the Republic. How much do they form of the population of Ireland as a whole?
        Is it   (a) 64%?
                (b) 74%?
                (c) 84%?

QUESTION 219

Who were the San Patricios?
      Were they   (a) the Irish battalion who fought for Mexico in the war of 1846-48 against the United States?
                (b) the Irish volunteers who fought for the Papal States between 1867 and 1870?
                (c) the 700 Irish who went to Spain to fight on the Nationalist side in the Spanish civil war?

ANSWER 216

(c) *Juno and the Paycock*. The "ay" sound in the vowel combination "ea" ("tay" for "tea", "paycock" for "peacock" is a survival of the pronunciation common in eighteenth-century England.

ANSWER 217

(c) 330 years. In 837 AD a probing fleet of sixty-five Viking ships sailed up the Liffey. By 841 the Vikings had established a permanent settlement, with a fortress on the high ground where the upper portion of Dublin Castle now stands. In 988 the Viking kingdom of Dublin was forced to pay tribute to Mael Seachlainn (*Anglice* Malachy), king of Meath. In 994 Malachy seized one of the city's most treasured possessions, the collar of Tomar, ancestor of the Norse kings of Dublin, an event commemorated by Thomas Moore: "*When Malachy wore the collar of gold/ Which he won from her proud invader* " ("Let Erin Remember the Days of Old"). The Vikings sought to free themselves from these exactions but were defeated decisively at the Battle of Clontarf in 1014. Nevertheless, Dublin was allowed to continue as a Viking-ruled kingdom within the Irish polity. The Viking era ended when the city fell to the next invaders, the Anglo-Normans, in 1171.

The Vikings also founded the sea-ports of Cork, Limerick, Waterford and Wexford. (The ending "-ford" comes from the Scandinavian *fiord*.) The Vikings, who were great European traders, specialised in ivory, furs and slaves. They ranged as far afield as Byzantium and Russia (the word Slav derives from the fact that the Slavonic peoples were a plentiful source of slaves). In Ireland, the Vikings became the leading traders and merchants. Around 1000 AD King Sitric III of Dublin minted the first Irish coins to facilitate commerce in what had become the greatest and most important Viking city outside Scandinavia.

ANSWER 218

(b) 74%, which compares with 94% for Spain, 88% for Portugal, 76% for Italy, 69% for France

ANSWER 219

(a) the Irish battalion who fought for Mexico. The San Patricio Battalion was composed mostly of Irish soldiers recruited by the US Army for the war but who, for reasons not clear, crossed the Rio Grande to join the Mexicans before hostilities began. They displayed exemplary bravery under fire, being finally reduced to a handful. After the last battle at Churubusco fifty of the survivors were hanged for desertion by the Americans. The executions caused outrage throughout Mexico and confirmed the San Patricios as national heroes. Their story has a place in history texts in Mexican schools. They are also commemorated by a monument, designed by the Mexican sculptor Lorenzo Rafael, in the town of San Angel near Mexico City.

QUESTION 220

The ancient Greeks speculated about the existence of atoms. The world of subatomic particles is a modern discovery. One of the major subatomic particles is the electron. An Irishman posited and named it sixteen years before it was shown by JJ Thomson of Cambridge to exist in fact .

Was he   (a) JG Stoney, honorary secretary of the Royal Dublin Society (the RDS) from 1871 to 1881?

(b) GF Fitzgerald, who in 1893 first put forward the explanation, now known as the Fitzgerald-Lorenz Contraction, which gives support to Einstein's Theory of Relativity?

(c) Sir William Rowan Hamilton (1805-65), mathematician and astronomer, whose greatest work *The Elements of Quaternions* was published the year after his death?

QUESTION 221

Anagram: W H O R E G D S E
Land borders

QUESTION 222

Tralee is the principal town in Kerry, the most hauntingly scenic part of Ireland. The beautiful song, "The Rose of Tralee", is based on fact and was written by a Munsterman.

Was he   (a) Gerald Griffin?

(b) William Pembroke Mulchinock?

(c) Francis Sylvester Mahony?

ANSWER 220

(a) JG Stoney, in 1881

ANSWER 221

Hedgerows. The patchwork of fields defined by hedgerows is a traditional and familiar feature of the Irish countryside. Hedgerows are man-made additions to the landscape, planted as a result of the Enclosure Acts beginning with the Cattle Act of 1667. Hawthorn was popular as a hedging plant because it could form a thick stockproof hedge in a short time. Since the enclosure period, other trees and shrubs have colonised the hedgerows, giving them the variety they have today. These strips of shrubby growth now provide leafy shelter and hidden habitats for many wild flowers, animals and birds. They are nature reserves in miniature. Since the 1950s hedgerows have been removed in vast amounts throughout Western Europe because of farm mechanisation. The destruction in Ireland, as the visitor can see, has been on a far smaller scale.

ANSWER 222

(b) William Pembroke Mulchinock (1820-64). Mulchinock, the son of a well-to-do Protestant merchant in Tralee, fell deeply in love with Mary O'Connor, the daughter of a poor Catholic shoemaker. He was twenty-three when he wrote his famous song for her in 1843. Unfortunately for them both, passions were running high as Daniel O'Connell's campaign to have the Act of Union (1800) repealed reached its peak. This Act had abolished the Irish parliament and provided for Irish representatives to sit at Westminster. Mulchinock espoused O'Connell's cause, and for breaking ranks with the local Ascendancy he was falsely charged with a political murder. He escaped arrest and ended up in India where he became a war correspondent. Six years were to pass before his name was cleared and he was able to return home in 1849, to claim his bride. But the Famine, though it ended in 1848, was still exacting its toll. Among its later victims was his beloved Mary, who had waited all those years for him. By a cruel irony, Mulchinock arrived home on the day of her funeral. Mulchinock never got over his tragic loss. He died at the age of forty-four and lies buried beside Mary, the first Rose of Tralee, in a graveyard not far from "the pure crystal fountain" of his song. Today, people come from all parts of the world every autumn to celebrate the festival of the Rose of Tralee.

QUESTION 223

The Céide Fields are a stretch of bogland outside Ballycastle on the north Mayo coast. Irish archaeologists have uncovered beneath it a unique site—the settlements and fields of a Neolithic farming community preserved exactly as they left them. Because the community intensively worked the soil, they gradually exhausted it and at length abandoned it to the encroaching bog. The bog finally engulfed the whole area, preserving it much as the lava from Vesuvius preserved Pompeii. How many years ago did the farming community work there?

> Is it   (a) 4,000?
>   (b) 5,000?
>   (c) 6,000?

QUESTION 224

Anagram: S K Y H E W I
The water of life

QUESTION 225

There is a wide range of goods that Ireland does not produce—cars, for example—and which it must therefore import. In 1991, the Republic spent 50% of its income on imports. Of imports in 1991, 41% came from the UK, 15% from the USA, 8% from Germany, 5% from Japan. Which category supplied the most imports?

> Was it   (a) consumption goods?
>   (b) materials for further processing?
>   (c) producers' capital goods?

QUESTION 226

Between the destruction of Clonmacnois in 1552 (founded as a seat of learning over one thousand years before, in 545 AD) and the Battle of the Boyne in 1690, the Irish established a network of some thirty colleges on the European mainland to educate their young men, mainly, but not exclusively, for the priesthood. This network extended from Lisbon to Prague and from Louvain to Rome. Which was the earliest college to be established?

> Was it   (a) Salamanca in Spain?
>   (b) Toulouse in France?
>   (c) St Isidore's in Rome?

ANSWER 223

(b) 5,000. There is an interpretative centre for visitors to the Céide Fields. "Céide" means a plateau in Irish.

ANSWER 224

whiskey, as it is spelt in Ireland and America (it is spelt whisky in Britain). The alembic, the still which was used in the Middle East to distil alcohol for perfumes, was introduced to Ireland in the sixth century. The Irish soon found a headier use for it—they invented whiskey. The word "whiskey" comes from the Irish and Scottish Gaelic words *uisce* (water) and *beatha* (life). It first came into the English language as *usquebaugh* ("water of life") in the sixteenth century. "Poteen" (pronounced "potcheen"), meaning illegal whiskey, and "shebeen" (an illegal drinking shop) are other words relating to drink which English has borrowed from Irish; both gained wide currency during Prohibition in the United States (1920-33). Irish whiskey, which is made from barley and water, is distilled at Old Bushmills Distillery in Bushmills, Co. Antrim, the oldest licensed whiskey distillery in the world (its licence dates back to 1608), and Midleton, Co.Cork, which, opened in 1975, is one of the most modern distilleries in the world. There are production differences between Irish and Scotch whiskey. Dr Johnson in his famous dictionary explained the difference in taste, "...the Irish sort is particularly distinguished for its pleasant and mild flavour. The Highland sort is somewhat hotter".

ANSWER 225

(b) materials for further processing (57% of the total). Consumption goods accounted for 28%, producers' capital goods (that is, machinery for producing goods) 14%. The Republic (1992) is the UK's sixth biggest customer after Germany, USA, France, the Netherlands and Italy; and it buys more from the UK than Australia, New Zealand, Canada and India combined.

ANSWER 226

(a) Salamanca, in 1582. With the destruction of many colleges during the French Revolution of 1789 and the founding of Maynooth College (the national seminary in Co. Kildare for students for the Catholic priesthood) in 1795, the era of these colleges had passed its zenith. In the 1820s France paid compensation for the losses incurred by the colleges during the Revolution. But they paid the money to the British government, which used part of it to build Marble Arch in London. Marble Arch is believed to be on the site of Tyburn Tree, where ironically St Oliver Plunkett, Archbishop of Armagh and an alumnus of the Irish College in Rome, was executed in 1681.

QUESTION 227

Who said, *"Property has its duties as well as its rights"*?
      Was it   (a) James Connolly?
               (b) Thomas Drummond?
               (c) Daniel O'Connell?

QUESTION 228

On the shortest day of the year, 21 December, the sun rises at 8.40 am and sets at 4.10 pm in the Dublin area, giving just 7 hours 30 minutes between the two times. What is the length of the longest day?
      Is it   (a) 15 hours?
             (b) 17 hours?
             (c) 19 hours?

QUESTION 229

Anagram: D E H L N A
German composer

QUESTION 230

The only person to win both the Nobel and Lenin peace prizes was an Irishman.
      Was he   (a) Éamon de Valera?
              (b) John A. Costello?
              (c) Seán MacBride?

ANSWER 227

(b) Thomas Drummond (1797-1840), in a letter to the third Earl of Donoughmore, who represented the landlords of Tippperary. Drummond, a Scot, was the Under-Secretary at Dublin Castle whose responsibilities included security. The landlords wished him to use military force against the tenant farmers in support of landlord rights. Drummond's concern for balance was well-founded: towards the end of the nineteenth century the break-down in the relationship between landlords and tenants resulted in the so-called "Land War", which ended with the transfer of ownership to the tenants through the mechanism of low-interest government loans. A statue of Drummond stands in Dublin's City Hall, on the base of which the famous quotation is inscribed.

ANSWER 228

(b) just over 17 hours. On the longest day, 21 June, the sun rises in Dublin about 4.54 am and sets about 9.57 pm. The summer evenings extend even later in the west of the country—sunset there is about twenty minutes behind Dublin. (Correspondingly, of course, sunrise is later in the west.) Summer Time currently (1994) operates in Ireland and Britain from the last Sunday in March until the last Sunday in October, a period of thirty weeks, and the times given here take account of that.

ANSWER 229

Handel, George Friedrich (1685-1759). One of the great mysteries of the history of music is the catastrophic decline in the eighteenth century of the native English talent for composition. (England had had about two and a half centuries of glorious achievement.) Foreign composers supplied the need. Of these, Handel, who arrived in England in 1710, was the most illustrious. Haydn called him "the master of us all". Handel's masterpiece, *The Messiah,* written in three weeks, was given its first performance in Dublin on 13 April 1742. It was conducted by the composer himself. The building in which it was performed no longer stands, but a plaque on the site in Fishamble Street, close to Dublin's Civic Offices, commemorates the transcendent event.

ANSWER 230

(c) Seán MacBride (1904-1988), Irish government minister (1948-51), chairman of Amnesty International (1961-75), and UN commissioner for Namibia (1974-76). He was the son of Maud Gonne, the inspiration of Yeats's love poems, and Major John MacBride, who fought against the British forces in the Boer War and who was executed for his part in the Easter Rising, 1916.

QUESTION 231

Anagram: S H E E N S Y N
A famous brand of brandy

QUESTION 232

What has been described as the greatest original Irish contribution to European literary themes is the notion of sudden, overwhelming love, lasting until death, that brings sorrow to the lovers. One of the earliest examples of such love is the story of Deirdre and the Sons of Uisneach. More widely known is the story of Tristan and Iseult, which has been part of the literature of Europe, in prose and poetry, for eight hundred years. Iseult (Ysut, Isolde) was the daughter of an Irish king: "On account of the daughter of the king of Ireland, Tristan engages them in battle" (*Por la fille au roi d'Irland/Offre Tristan vers eus batalle*). Dante (1265-1321) in the *Inferno* recounts seeing Tristan in the second circle of Hades in the company of Helen, Achilles and other tragic lovers. The story of the two lovers is a recurring theme in many French romances; it appears in Sir Thomas Malory's *Morte d'Arthur* (1469), the last medieval rendering of the Arthurian legend; it is the subject of Wagner's opera, *Tristan and Isolde* (1865); and it is used by Tennyson in his *Idylls of the King*. Where in Ireland is there a place bearing Iseult's name?

Is it in   (a) Co. Armagh?
            (b) Co. Dublin?
            (c) Co. Meath?

QUESTION 233

Who said, "*No man has the right to fix the boundary to the march of a nation. No man has a right to say to his country 'Thus far shalt thou go and no further'. We have never attempted to fix the 'ne plus ultra' to the progress of Ireland's nationhood—and we never shall*"?

Was it   (a) Daniel O'Connell?
         (b) Charles Stewart Parnell?
         (c) Éamon de Valera?

QUESTION 234

Menapia is the Latin name of an Irish seaport. The name was recorded by the Greco-Egyptian geographer Ptolemy. The port was called after the Menapii, a Celtic tribe from Belgium.

Was the seaport (a) Waterford?
                (b) Wexford?
                (c) Wicklow?

ANSWER 231

Hennessy. Hennessy Cognac was founded in 1765 by a Corkman, Richard Hennessy, who had gone to France in 1740 to join the Irish Brigade.The Hennessys in France, like the Guinnesses in Ireland, became a powerful commercial dynasty. Louis Vuitton Moët Hennessy—the group's interests extend beyond brandy to Christian Dior scents, Roc beauty products and the Luxembourg Television network among others—is the biggest luxury item group in France. By a curious coincidence, the names Hennessy and Guinness derive from the same ancestral name. Hennessy (Ó hAonghusa) means descendant of Aonghus and Guinness (Mac Aonghusa) means son of Aonghus. Aonghus was the son of the Dagda, the chief of the earliest Irish gods, and Boand, the goddess after whom the River Boyne is called. By an even more curious coincidence the Guinness company is now a significant shareholder in Louis Vuitton Moët Hennessy.

ANSWER 232

(b) Co. Dublin. Chapelizod (Séipéal Íosóid), meaning Iseult's Chapel, is a village on the Liffey on the western edge of Dublin's Phoenix Park. Joyce in *Finnegans Wake* sites HC Earwicker's pub there.

ANSWER 233

(b) Charles Stewart Parnell (1846-91), "the uncrowned King of Ireland" and one of the most brilliant tacticians ever to appear at Westminster. He made the statement in 1886 when the great Liberal British Prime Minister WE Gladstone pressed him as to whether or not the proposed Home Rule Bill would satisfy utterly Irish nationalist aspirations. The words are inscribed on the Parnell monument at the upper end of O'Connell Street, Dublin.

ANSWER 234

(b) Wexford

QUESTION 235

Anagram: A F R I C E
A four-wheeled vehicle and an Irish saint

QUESTION 236

Arthur Conan Doyle (1859-1930), the creator of Sherlock Holmes, born in Scotland, was of Irish descent—Conan is a traditional Irish first name and Doyle is an Irish surname. He often gave lectures on the exploits of the Irish Brigade in the service of France and delighted in recounting an episode from the glory days of the Brigade in the first half of the eighteenth century in which the French king met with a group of Irish officers to convey the complaints of his French generals: "They tell me you Irish give more trouble than any other corps". One of the Irish colonels responded, "That complaint is nothing new, Sire. Your enemies have made it a hundred times before". By the 1760s there were few Irish rank-and-file recruits to the Irish Brigade. The British were then successfully recruiting in Ireland although they did not enlist Catholic officers—those still went to France. Thus in 1770 Captain Daniel O'Conor wrote of the Brigade: "...a band of ruffians and cut-throats...a vile mob of hirelings, a medley of all the nations of Europe, the excrement of the human race... Perhaps there is not one tenth part of us genuine Irish" (*The O'Conor Papers*). Which Irish poet wrote:

> *... in far foreign fields from Dunkirk to Belgrade*
> *Lie the soldiers and chiefs of the Irish Brigade* ?

Was it   (a) James Clarence Mangan?
          (b) Thomas Moore?
          (c) Thomas Davis?

QUESTION 237

Which Italian composer, a contemporary of the Irish composer and harpist, Turlough Carolan (1670-1738), described him as *"a true genius of music "* (*il genio vero della musica*)?

Was it   (a) Arcangelo Corelli (1653-1713)?
          (b) Antonio Vivaldi (*c.*1675-1741)?
          (c) Francesco Geminiani (*c.*1685-1762)?

ANSWER 235

Fiacre. St Fiachra, who died *c*.670, founded a hostel in France for Irish pilgrims which later grew into the monastery of Breuil in the district of Paris now known as Saint-Fiacre. His remains were placed in an ornate shrine in 1234. In 1422 King Henry IV of England threatened to remove the remains to London as a reprisal against the Irish who were then opposing him in the French army. But before he could do so, he sickened with haemorrhoids (the *mal de St Fiacre*) and died on the saint's feast day! The vehicle takes its name from the Hôtel de St Fiacre in Paris, where they were first hired out.

ANSWER 236

(c) Thomas Davis (1814–45), a key figure in Irish nationalism. He was a leader of the nineteenth-century Young Ireland movement. A statue of Davis by Edward Delaney stands in Dame Street, Dublin, facing Trinity College, where he was educated. Delaney's statue of Wolfe Tone (1763–98), the leading ideologist of the United Irishmen, who persuaded the Directory in Paris to send two fleets in support of the United Irishmen, stands at the corner of St Stephen's Green Dublin, near the Shelbourne Hotel.

ANSWER 237

(c) Francesco Geminiani, a pupil of Corelli's, who settled in London, where he made an immense contribution to English violin technique. One of Carolan's sons, who in 1747 also went to London, where he taught the Irish harp, published a collection of his father's music under the patronage of Dr Delany, a close friend of Swift. Charles O'Conor, a contemporary of Carolan's and a descendant of the last High King of Ireland (Rory O'Connor, who died in 1198), said of Carolan, "The Italian compositions he preferred to all others; Vivaldi charmed him, and with Corelli he was enraptured". Oliver Goldsmith recounts the following story: "Being once at the house of an Irish nobleman, where there was a musician present, who was eminent in the profession, Carolan immediately challenged him to a trial of skill. To carry the jest forward, his Lordship persuaded the musician to accept the challenge, and he accordingly played on his fiddle the fifth concerto of Vivaldi. Carolan, immediately taking his harp, played over the whole piece after him, without missing a note, though he had never heard it before, which produced some surprise; but their astonishment increased when he assured them he could make a concerto in the same taste himself, which he instantly composed". Carolan's Concerto is still a favourite.

QUESTION 238

Where in Ireland was the Welsh language in continuous use, for over one hundred years, until 1939?

Was it in   (a) Rosslare?
               (b) Howth?
               (c) Dublin?

QUESTION 239

Irish traditional music has had a formative influence on American country and western music. In recent decades it has stimulated a phenomenal folk music movement in one of the following European countries.

Is it   (a) Italy?
          (b) Sweden?
          (c) Germany?

QUESTION 240

Oscar Wilde once said of a fellow-Irishman, *"He hasn't an enemy in the world, and none of his friends likes him."*

Did he say it of   (a) Charles Stewart Parnell?
                   (b) George Russell (AE)?
                   (c) George Bernard Shaw?

QUESTION 241

How many members do the people of Ireland send to the European Parliament?

Is it   (a) 12?
          (b) 16?
          (c) 18?

QUESTION 242

Which Irish poet wrote of a schoolmaster and his pupils:

> *Well had the boding tremblers learned to trace*
> *The day's disasters in his morning face;*
> *Full well they laughed with counterfeited glee,*
> *At all his jokes, for many a joke had he?*

Was it   (a) WB Yeats?
           (b) Oliver Goldsmith?
           (c) Patrick Kavanagh?

ANSWER 238

(c) Dublin. In 1831 a chapel was founded in Poolbeg Street specifically for Welsh speakers. The services were moved in 1839 to Bethel Chapel, in Talbot Street. A smaller chapel, Bethel Bach (Little Bethel) existed for a time at Dún Laoghaire (then Kingstown) for sailors. The last service in Welsh was conducted in Bethel in 1939, one week before the outbreak of World War II.

ANSWER 239

(c) Germany. *Volksmusik* now occupies up to five hours in prime slots on German weekend television. The *Volksmusik* movement began in the seventies when The Chieftains and other traditional Irish groups toured Germany and created a vogue for Irish folk music. When the supply of Irish artists could not keep up with the demand, German artists stepped in. They began to set German lyrics to Irish tunes and eventually reached back into their own folk traditions.

ANSWER 240

(c) George Bernard Shaw, as quoted by Shaw in *Sixteen Self Sketches*

ANSWER 241

(c) 18 (15 are returned by the Republic, 3 by Northern Ireland). Labour and the Social Democratic Labour Party (SDLP) are attached to the largest group in the European Parliament, the Party of European Socialists. Fine Gael and the Ulster Unionists are attached to the European People's Party (Christian Democratic) Group. The Progressive Democrats are attached to the Liberal Democratic and Reformist Group. Fianna Fáil is attached to the European Democratic Alliance. Independent Fianna Fáil is attached to the Rainbow Group. The Democratic Left and the Democratic Unionist Party are non-attached.

ANSWER 242

(b) Oliver Goldsmith (1728-74), in *The Deserted Village*. In "Retaliation", Goldsmith wrote of his fellow-Irishman Edmund Burke:

> *Here lies our good Edmund, whose genius was such,*
> *We scarcely can praise it, or blame it too much;*
> *Who, born for the Universe, narrowed his mind,*
> *And to party gave up what was meant for mankind.*

Goldsmith's statue stands near Burke's in front of Trinity College Dublin. Both were graduates of the college.

QUESTION 243

During the penal times, when Catholic education was severely inhibited, an independent system of basic first and second level education, known as "hedge-schools", spread throughout Ireland. When was this system at its height?

Was it   (a) between 1600 and 1750?
           (b) between 1650 and 1800?
           (c) between 1700 and 1850?

QUESTION 244

The great socialist anthem *The Red Flag* ("Though cowards flinch and traitors jeer,/ We'll keep the Red Flag flying here!") was written by an Irishman.

Was he   (a) James Connell (1850-1929)?
          (b) James Connolly (1870-1916)?
          (c) Pádraig Ó Conaire (1882-1928)?

QUESTION 245

An Irish priest served as Louis XVI's confessor on the eve of his execution and accompanied him to the scaffold on 21 January 1793.

Was he   (a) Dr Patrick Plunkett?
          (b) Dr Charles Kearney?
          (c) Abbé Henry Essex Edgeworth?

QUESTION 246

St Brendan, who died *c*.580, was famous for his exploratory voyages into the Atlantic. An account of these was written by Irish monks in Latin *c*.950—the last major work by Irish scribes in that language. Entitled *Navigatio Sancti Brendani Abbatis*, the book became in effect a medieval bestseller, and stimulated the curiosity about the Atlantic which eventually led to the discovery of America by Europeans. The work was especially popular in vernacular translations in the Low Countries and Germany. Devotion to the saint was particularly strong in the German marches along the Baltic. When the territory around Branibor was taken from the Slavs by Lothair, Duke of Saxony, in 1106, it was named Brandenburg after the saint. Thus today one of the most famous monuments in the world, the Brandenburg Gate in Berlin, in the heart of Europe, has an unexpected link with the daring sixth-century monk born on the western seaboard of Ireland. In what county was St Brendan born?

Was it   (a) Sligo?
          (b) Mayo?
          (c) Kerry?

ANSWER 243

(c) between 1700 and 1850. An official enquiry in 1713 revealed that there were some 560 "Papist" schools (most of them illegal) functioning in every diocese in Ireland except Derry. A survey in 1824 showed that there were 9,300 hedge-schools with 400,000 pupils. When the National School system was introduced *c.*1830 the hedge-schools went into decline; however the last of them lingered on until the beginning of the twentieth century in Connacht. Although the term "hedge-school" connoted contempt, the standard of education provided by the best of them could be high. Among those who were educated by hedge-school masters were Oliver Goldsmith, who has left a memorable account of his village schoolmaster in *The Deserted Village*, Edmund Ignatius Rice, who in 1820 founded the Christian Brothers; William Carleton, the novelist; and Edmund Burke's maternal relations. Progress towards a national system of public education in Britain was slower than in Ireland: it was not until 1870 that local school boards were established which could compel school attendance up to thirteen years of age. More rapid progress was hindered there, partly by a clash between Church and Dissent, and partly by lack of widespread public interest, since children were a source of cheap labour for factory and mill owners, and an additional source of income for the poor.

ANSWER 244

(a) James Connell. Born in Co. Meath, Connell was a radical Irish nationalist. When he was nearly forty, he went to live in London where he became secretary of the Workmen's Legal Friendly Society. He wrote the song during the great dock strike of 1889. It was published in the socialist magazine *Justice* and in 1895 was set to the rousing old German air "Tannenbaum".

ANSWER 245

(c) Abbé Henry Essex Edgeworth (1745-1807). A relation of the novelist Maria Edgeworth (her father was his cousin), the priest had been for a few years previously the confessor of Madame Elizabeth, the king's sister. After the king's execution, Edgeworth made his way towards the ranks of armed soldiers massed around the scaffold. These, to his great relief, opened to let him through and he was soon lost among the crowd.

ANSWER 246

(c) Kerry. One of the loftiest mountains there commands an eternal view of the Atlantic. It is called Mount Brandon.

The Gap of Dunloe, Killarney

INDEX